Arden L. Hodgins, Jr.

Great God of Wonders

GREAT GOD
of
WONDERS

The attributes of God

Peter Jeffery

 EVANGELICAL PRESS

EVANGELICAL PRESS
12 Wooler Street, Darlington, Co. Durham, DL1 1RQ, England

© Evangelical Press 1993
First published 1993

British Library Cataloguing in Publication Data available

ISBN 0 85234 302 7

Printed and bound in Great Britain at Cox & Wyman Ltd., Reading.

Contents

Introduction

When we first become Christians we are understandably thrilled with the Lord Jesus Christ and what he did for us on the cross. Also, to a degree, we appreciate that we could never have been saved without the work of the Holy Spirit. So often our total understanding of the great triune God of Scripture is only of the Son and of the Spirit, and the majesty and glory of God the Father remain a mystery as yet unfathomed. Sadly, for many believers this situation hardly changes throughout the whole of their Christian lives.

This book is written to help those beginning the Christian faith to see something of the attributes of God. Any study of God will of necessity remain incomplete because the more we learn, the more there is to learn. Still, such a study should be exciting and satisfying for a young Christian. What can be more exciting than discovering biblical truths about God, and what can be more satisfying than to have our minds and hearts enlarged by the knowledge of God?

There are many fine books on the attributes of God but I have drawn mainly on three: *Knowing God* by J. I. Packer, *The Knowledge of the Holy* by A. W. Tozer and *The Attributes of God* by A.W. Pink.

1.
The attributes of God

Dr Tozer defines an attribute of God as 'whatever God has revealed as being true of himself'. God has revealed himself in Scripture and there we find that he is sovereign and holy. He is a God of providence and patience and many other attributes. If we were to ask the question, 'What is God like?' the answer of Scripture would be that he is not like anything at all. He is so gloriously unique that any attempt on our part to define God, apart from what he has revealed, will inevitably result in idolatry. Tozer wrote, 'The essence of idolatry is the entertainment of thoughts about God that are unworthy of him.' He added, 'Among the sins to which the human heart is prone, hardly any other is more hateful to God than idolatry, for idolatry is at bottom a libel of His character. The idolatrous heart assumes that God is other than He is — in itself a monstrous sin — and substitutes for the true God one made after its own likeness. Always this god will conform to the image of the one who created it and it will be base or pure, cruel or kind, according to the moral state of the mind from which it emerges.'[1]

It is crucial, therefore, that we confine our thoughts about God to what he teaches about himself in Scripture. This avoids the fatal mistake of formulating our doctrine of God more by sentiment than truth. So often you hear people say, 'I believe in a God of love, and he would never judge people or cast them into hell.' The Bible certainly teaches that love is an attribute of God, but so too are wrath and justice. These are not incompatible but are all part of the being of God.

We shall begin by considering three reasons why it is important for Christians to study the biblical teaching on who and what God is.

Firstly, *it will help to avoid the ignorance of God that seems to plague so much of modern Christianity*. There is a tendency in most people to think of God in terms of their own limitations. So if we cannot do something, neither can God. Thus the Almighty God of Scripture is reduced to manageable terms and Christianity is emptied of its very uniqueness, namely the supernatural power of God. A. W. Pink makes a similar point: 'The god of this twentieth century no more resembles the Supreme Sovereign of Holy Writ than does the dim flickering of a candle resemble the glory of the midday sun.'[2]

Secondly, on a more positive note, the study of God is the highest and greatest subject that can occupy the mind of a Christian. It is the most stimulating, most exciting, most satisfying and most comforting of subjects. Charles Spurgeon, when he was only twenty years old, said, 'Nothing will so enlarge the intellect, nothing so magnify the whole soul of man, as a devout, earnest, continued investigation of the great subject of the Deity... Would you lose your sorrow? Would you drown your cares? Then go, plunge yourself in the Godhead's deepest sea, be lost in His immensity; and you shall come forth as from a couch of rest refreshed and invigorated.'[3]

Thirdly, many Christians believe that the only answer to the godlessness and unbelief of today is a God-sent revival. *The greatest stimulus to pray for revival is to appreciate the greatness and power of God.*

Discovering God

We often say to unbelievers that it is one thing to *know about* God and another to *know* God. That is true, but it is also true that once a person knows God as Father and Saviour, he or she will want to go on to discover as much as possible about God.

And the more we learn about God, the more we shall appreciate him and love him. This is why God has revealed himself in Scripture.

When a man is first saved he may know very little about God. He knows he is a sinner and that God sent his Son to save sinners. He knows of the love and mercy of God, and that is enough for salvation. Then he starts living the Christian life and from the Bible he discovers that God is holy. This humbles him and fills him with a sense of wonder that the holy God should accept him, a vile sinner. The result is a greater love for God. Then he discovers, again from Scripture, the sovereignty of God — that God planned his salvation before the foundation of the world. This leaves him speechless, but it also leaves an indelible mark of devotion and thanks to God.

As this man goes on in the faith he comes across the providence of God — that God is caring for him and providing for his every need. He is not subject to luck or chance, but to a divine providence.

Then at some point he will know failure and defeat in his Christian life. Sin triumphs, and in his sense of guilt he discovers the patience and long-suffering of God. He may then find himself in an impossible situation. All things are against him and he feels helpless; at that point he experiences the power of God working for him.

What is happening to this Christian? He is discovering the attributes of God, of which he knew nothing at salvation. They humble him, but they also thrill him and he loves God even more. The attributes of God do not belong to the realm of theory; they are not mere doctrines that have no bearing upon the Christian's daily living. Rather they are most practical and enriching.

Strength in knowledge

Nowhere does the Bible regard salvation as an end in itself. Salvation is always the beginning. The knowledge we receive of God at conversion is only the key that opens up the possibility of knowing God in all his fulness. This knowledge of the fulness of God is essential to a strong and healthy Christian life. While it is true that head-knowledge of God without heart-knowledge is useless, it is also true that God never meant us to have only heart-knowledge. The Bible urges us to learn, to think, to study, to understand God, and there is spiritual strength in such knowledge.

We can know of God only what he has chosen to reveal in Scripture, but what he has revealed we need to know. Listen to Jeremiah 9:23-24:

> 'This is what the Lord says:
>> "Let not the wise man boast of his wisdom
>> or the strong man boast of his strength
>> or the rich man boast of his riches,
>> but let him who boasts boast about this:
>>> that he understands and knows me,
>> that I am the Lord, who exercises kindness,
>>> justice and righteousness on the earth,
>>> for in these I delight,"
>
> declares the Lord.'

Wisdom, strength and riches are the things the natural man always boasts of, and they are three traps the devil uses to ensnare us. How can we avoid these pitfalls? By glorying in the understanding and knowledge of God. This means to have a correct insight into the nature and being of God, and to act in keeping with such an understanding. It means that we delight in what God delights in — kindness, justice and righteousness. We fill our minds with the knowledge of God, so that our hearts can be filled with the joy of serving and pleasing God. Such knowledge will produce godliness and there is no greater strength than this.

Godliness will lead to victory and triumph instead of

constant defeat. Daniel 11:32 tells us that the people who know their God shall be strong (see the AV). Why did Shadrach, Meshach and Abednego defy King Nebuchadnezzar? Because they knew their God (Daniel 3:17). Why was Daniel unafraid to enter the lions' den? Because he knew and trusted God (Daniel 6:22). Dr Packer said that those who know God have great energy for God, great thoughts of God, great boldness for God and great contentment in God.[4]

It is the Christian's supreme privilege to know God: therefore we ought to set ourselves to learn to know him.

2.
The sovereignty of God

By the sovereignty of God we mean the absolute rule of God and his authority over all creation. This is a rule which covers everything without exception — creation, animals, weather, man and man's salvation. A. W. Pink says, 'Divine sovereignty means that God is God in fact, as well as in name, that He is on the throne of the universe, directing all things, working all things "after the counsel of His own will".'[1]

God is sovereign because he is God. He is not like us, cumbered about with all sorts of limitations and restrictions. Any understanding of God that limits his sovereignty will cause us serious problems in our understanding of his other attributes. Dr Packer points out that 'Today, vast stress is laid on the thought that God is *personal*, but this truth is so stated as to leave the impression that God is a person of the same sort as we are — weak, inadequate, ineffective, a little pathetic. But this is not the God of the Bible! Our personal life is a finite thing; it is limited in every direction, in space, in time, in knowledge, in power. But God is not so limited. He is eternal, infinite, and almighty. He has us in His hands; but we never have Him in ours. Like us, He is personal, but unlike us He is great.'[2]

There is always this tendency in man to think of God as no more than an extension of himself. In Psalm 50:21, God accuses a rebellious and sinful Israel, 'You thought I was altogether like you.' To think of God as a man, albeit the

greatest of men, will always result in limiting God. Jesus'
question, 'Who do men say I am?' brought forth the answers:
'John the Baptist, Elijah, Jeremiah.' These were high opinions
of the Saviour, but fell far short of the truth. Martin Luther once
accused the great Bible scholar Erasmus, 'Your thoughts of
God are too human.' And that was one reason why Erasmus
was never any more than a great scholar while Luther, with his
eyes on the sovereign God, was used to set the world ablaze
with the Reformation.

Absolute rule

The absolute sovereignty of God is plainly taught in Scripture:

> 'Yours, O Lord, is the greatness and the power
>   and the glory and the majesty and the splendour,
>   for everything in heaven and earth is yours.
> Yours, O Lord, is the kingdom:
>   You are exalted as head over all.
> Wealth and honour come from you;
>   you are the ruler of all things.
> In your hands are strength and power
>   to exalt and give strength to all'
>
> (1 Chronicles 29:11-12).

'O Lord, God of our fathers, are you not the God who is in
heaven? You rule over all the kingdoms of the nations. Power
and might are in your hand, and no one can withstand you' (2
Chronicles 20:6).

Before such a God kings and rulers and all men are nothing.
Christians need to remember that this is our God. This is the
God who has loved us and saved us. The God of the Bible is no
fairy-tale king, but the sovereign Lord. Job tells us, 'He stands
alone, and who can oppose him? He does whatever he pleases'
(Job 23:13).

God's supremacy over creation is demonstrated over and over again in Scripture. At his will the Red Sea opened (Exodus 14); the sun stood still (Joshua 10) and even moved backwards (Isaiah 38). This is our God, sovereign and almighty. 'I know that the Lord is great... The Lord does whatever pleases him' (Psalm 135:5-6). To say that God is sovereign must mean that he rules. He does not merely look on as an interested spectator, but actually rules. This God, who never slumbers or sleeps, is at any given moment in full control of the affairs of the world. He reigns, not with his hands tied behind his back awaiting the co-operation and permission of men, but as the Almighty One. Nothing is impossible for him. This is how God is presented in the Bible. Is this how we see him? It is true that there is much that we do not understand, do not like and do not want, but that must not affect our understanding of God.

Problems

The obvious problem is that we do not see God's rule in the world today. The world is an ungodly place where God's laws are rejected and ridiculed. Evil and sin seem to dominate with no serious challenge. James Montgomery Boice answers this problem with these words: 'The explanation of the seeming contradiction is that human rebellion, while it is in opposition to God's express command, falls within His eternal or hidden purpose. That is, God permits sin for His own reasons, knowing in advance that He will bring sin to judgement in the day of His wrath and that in the meantime it will not go beyond the bounds that He has fixed for it. Many things work against the sovereignty of God — from our perspective. But from God's perspective, His decrees are always established. They are, in fact, as the *Westminster Shorter Catechism* describes them, "His eternal purpose, according to the counsel of His will whereby, for His own glory, He hath foreordained whatsoever comes to pass".'[3]

Comfort

It should be clear by this point in human history that man has no answer to sin. Education, philosophy, morality, or even prosperity, do not change man's cruelty, envy and greed. The atrocities committed by man in the twentieth century show that sin's grip on human nature is as strong as ever. Sin would reign unchallenged were it not for the sovereignty of God. God does not only condemn sin, he defeats it and one day will eradicate it completely. This is why, though the Christian on occasions will have problems with this doctrine, when he really begins to understand it, he discovers that it is the most comforting of doctrines. Then he will agree with Spurgeon that 'There is no attribute more comforting to His children than that of God's sovereignty. Under the most adverse circumstances, in the most severe trials, they believe that sovereignty has ordained their afflictions, that sovereignty overrules them, and that sovereignty will sanctify them all. There is nothing for which the children ought more earnestly to contend than the doctrine of the Kingship of God over all the works of His own hands — the Throne of God and His right to sit upon that Throne.'[4]

In chapter 40 of the book of Isaiah the prophet seeks to bring comfort to a troubled and confused people, and he does it by reminding them of the sovereignty of God. 'Here God speaks to people whose mood is the mood of many Christians today — despondent people, cowed people, secretly despairing people; people against whom the tide of events has been running for a very long time; people who have ceased to believe that the cause of Christ can ever prosper again.'[5]

Twice the prophet rebukes the people for forgetting who God is:

'Do you not know?
    Have you not heard?'

(Isaiah 40: 21-28).

Following both rebukes he immediately reminds them of the
sovereign power of God:

> 'He sits enthroned above the circle of the earth...
> The Lord is the everlasting God,
>   the Creator of the ends of the earth.
> He will not grow tired or weary.'

The great cry of Isaiah in verse 9 is, 'Here is your God,' and
he calls them to look and consider who God is.

Look at *creation* (v. 12). It is so vast, yet God made it and
controls it.

Look at *the nations* (v. 15). No matter what century we live
in, there will always be some great power that dominates
others, but even the greatest is nothing, a mere drop in a bucket,
compared with the power of God.

Look at *the world* (v. 22). It dwarfs us, yet God dwarfs it.
Then go outside the world and look at *the stars*. The heavens
are majestic and awesome, and we can well understand David's
wonder in Psalm 8 — What is man compared to this? Yet, says
verse 26, who created all these? This verse brings before us a
thrilling description of the sovereign power of God:

> 'He … brings out the starry host one by one,
>   and calls them each by name.
> Because of his great power and mighty strength
>   not one of them is missing.'

This God is incomparable (v. 25). See what hope and
comfort we can justifiably expect from him:

> 'He gives strength to the weary
>   and increases the power of the weak.
> Even youths grow tired and weary,
>   and young men stumble and fall;

but those who hope in the Lord
    will renew their strength.
They will soar on wings like eagles;
    they will run and not grow weary.
they will walk and not be faint'

(vv. 29-31).

Christian, this is your God. He is sovereign, and because this is so peace and confidence should always mark our Christian lives. The only ground for optimism in this world is that our God reigns.

3.
The sovereignty of God in salvation

In the last chapter we touched upon some of the problems Christians have with the doctrine of the sovereignty of God. By far the greatest problem arises, for some, when we think of this doctrine in relationship to man's salvation. The sovereignty of God in salvation is commonly known as the doctrine of election and it has been the source of great controversy in the church. For instance, John Wesley vigorously denied the doctrine, while Charles Spurgeon said, 'I do not believe we can preach the Gospel if we do not preach justification by faith, without works; nor unless we preach the Sovereignty of God in His dispensation of grace; nor unless we exalt the electing, unchangeable, eternal, immutable, conquering love of Jehovah; nor do I think we can preach the Gospel, unless we base it upon the special and particular redemption of His elect and chosen people which Christ wrought out upon the Cross.'[1]

We need to be clear as to what this doctrine is saying. So let us first take a definition of election from William Hendriksen: 'Election may be defined as God's eternal purpose to cause certain specific individuals to be in Christ the recipients of special grace, in order that they may live to God's glory and may obtain everlasting salvation.'[2] These things can only be true if God is a sovereign God. Election in salvation simply means that God saves specific individuals. Dr Packer puts it as follows: 'God saves sinners. *God* — the Triune Jehovah, Father, Son and Spirit, Three Persons working together in sovereign wisdom, power and love to achieve the salvation of a chosen people, the Father electing, the Son fulfilling the Father's will by redeeming, the Spirit executing the purpose of Father and Son by renewing. *Saves* — does everything, first to last, that is involved in bringing man from death in sin to life in glory; plans, achieves and communicates redemption, calls and keeps, justifies, sanctifies, glorifies. *Sinners* — men as God finds them, guilty, vile, helpless, powerless, unable to lift a finger to do God's will or better their spiritual lot. God saves sinners.'[3]

Children of promise

There are many passages in Scripture that we could go to in studying this truth, but we will confine ourselves primarily to Romans 9. The amazing thing about this chapter is the clarity and simplicity of the argument.

No one is a child of God because of birth or nationality. It is God who makes us his children. Paul makes a distinction between natural children and children of promise. He illustrates this in verse 9 by showing God's attitude to Abraham's two sons. Ishmael was the child of nature, but Isaac's birth would have been impossible naturally because his mother Sarah was well past the age of child-bearing. Isaac was the child of promise, the product solely of sovereign power and love. The result of this was that God rejected Ishmael, and divine blessing came upon Isaac and ultimately on his descendants. The point of comparison between Isaac and believers today is that Christians too are children of promise. They became God's children, not by natural birth, but by divine intervention. They are born again as a result of the activity of God the Holy Spirit (read Galatians 4:21-31). Our spiritual birth is not due to anything in us, but entirely to the sovereign will of God.

So far so good, most Christians would agree with this. But Paul does not stop there. In Romans 9:10 he says, 'not only that'; he wants to make it clear that God chooses his people solely on terms of sovereign grace. In case it may be assumed God chose Isaac because his mother was the legitimate wife of Abraham and Ishmael's mother was not, we are given an example that removes this doubt. Ishmael was the result of sinful scheming by Abraham and Sarah (Genesis 16:1-4), but nothing like this surrounded the birth of Jacob and Esau. They were both born in answer to prayer (Genesis 25:21). They were both born to Rebekah, the legitimate wife of Isaac. They were twins and everything about them was similar, but 'Before the twins were born or had done anything good or bad — in order that God's purpose in election might stand: not by works but by him who calls — she was told, "The older will serve the younger." Just as it is written: "Jacob I loved, but Esau I hated"' (Romans 9:11-13). This took place before the children were born — so there is no question of one being better than the other and therefore deserving God's favour. The only reason given for God's choice is that it was 'in order that God's purpose in election might stand'. William Hendriksen sums up verses 6-13 in these words: 'In the final analysis the reason why some people are accepted and others rejected is that God so willed it... Human responsibility is not cancelled, but there is no such thing as human merit. God's eternal purpose is not ultimately based on human works.'[4]

The position of man's salvation is stated simply in Romans 9:15-18. It rests in God's hands. This is the clear teaching of Paul in Romans 9 and is exactly what Jesus taught in John 6:44, where he said, 'No one can come to me unless the Father who sent me draws him,' and John 17:6, where, addressing his Father, he speaks of 'those whom you gave me out of the world. They were yours; you gave them to me and they have obeyed your word.'

Objections

Paul anticipates two objections to this teaching. The first, in verse 14, says, 'This is not fair.' The second, in verse 19, says, 'If this is true it removes human responsibility.' It is interesting that the same two objections are constantly raised two thousand years later.

Paul first answers the objection that it is not fair that God should choose one and not another. God does not punish anyone unfairly. All are sinners and all deserve God's wrath. God did not make Pharaoh a sinner, any more than he made us sinners. We are sinners by nature and this works itself out in our actions. But God in his mercy saves some, and in his justice condemns others. Therefore the one saved can never say, 'I am better than others,' and the one condemned must acknowledge that he receives no more than what his sin deserves.

As to the question of man's responsibility, voiced in the objection, 'Why does God blame us?' Paul says such thinking springs from an ignorance of the true relationship between God and man. Who are we to talk back to God and seek to bring God before the bar of man's justice and reasoning? Who are we, with our minds warped by sin, to dare to criticize God? Man is responsible for his own sin, but 'The guilty sinner constantly tries to evade any sense of personal responsibility, yet all the time he knows that he is responsible for his actions, and will have to answer for them at the judgement. The height of this wickedness is that he will even make the sovereign election of God a reason why he should not be answerable for his actions — although God declares in his Word, with equal dogmatism, that all men will be held responsible for everything they think, or say or do.'[5]

No one can give all the answers about the sovereignty of God in salvation, but it is clearly taught in Scripture, and there is no doctrine so humbling, so thrilling, so stimulating to praise and worship, nor any doctrine that so encourages evangelism.

4.
The foreknowledge of God

In looking at the foreknowledge of God we are still in a sense dealing with God's sovereignty, because many Christians who do not accept election reject it on their interpretation of his foreknowledge. They appeal to a verse like 1 Peter 1:2, which is addressed to to those 'who have been chosen [elect] according to the foreknowledge of God the Father,' and from this they deduce that God foresaw, before the world was created, who would believe and respond to the gospel and on this basis God elected some to salvation. This seems to remove the problem of God being unfair and also that of man's responsibility, but it is significant that in Romans 9, when he is dealing with these objections to election, Paul does not argue that the objectors have misunderstood him and that all he means is that God foresaw what would happen and acted accordingly. Paul does not do that because he does not interpret foreknowledge in this way. As A. W. Pink points out, such an interpretation would take 'away the independency of God for it makes His decrees rest upon what he discovers in the creature'.[1]

More than omniscience

God's omniscience means that God knows all things. There is nothing unknown or hidden to Almighty God. The Bible is full of this great truth:

'You know when I sit and when I rise;
   you perceive my thoughts from afar.
You discern my going out and my lying down;
   you are familiar with all my ways.
Before a word is on my tongue
   you know it completely, O Lord'

(Psalm 139:2-4).

'Nothing in all creation is hidden from God's sight. Everything is uncovered and laid bare before the eyes of him to whom we must give account' (Hebrews 4:13).

This is glorious and breathtaking, but foreknowledge means more than omniscience. Here is God not merely knowing, but doing. Foreknowledge implies certainty, and certainty implies foreordination or predestination. John Murray argues it means 'whom he set regard upon,' or 'whom he knew from eternity with distinguishing affection and delight,' and is virtually equivalent to 'whom he foreloved. It is sovereign distinguishing love.' Is Murray correct? What does the Bible mean by foreknowledge?

The word is not found in the Old Testament, but the verb 'to know' is, and when it is used to describe God's relationship to man it carries a very special meaning. For instance, in Jeremiah 1:5 the Lord tells Jeremiah, 'Before I formed you in the womb I knew you.' In this verse the verb means much more than to know about; it carries says, A. W. Pink, the meaning of loved or appointed. Dr Lloyd-Jones says, 'When we read in Scripture that God knows someone or certain people, it means that he has a special interest in them, that he has set his love upon them, that he is planning and has purposed certain things with respect to them.'[2]

The same is true in the New Testament. Jesus said in Matthew 7:23, 'Then I will tell them plainly, "I never knew you. Away from me, you evildoers." To know, in this verse, is obviously more than omniscience. Jesus means by saying he never knew them, that they never belonged to him, were never his people, never had a special and peculiar saving relationship to him.

New Testament usage

Foreknowledge is found five times in the New Testament and each time the context makes it clear that it means foreordination or predestination.

Acts 2:23. 'This man was handed over to you by God's set purpose and foreknowledge; and you, with the help of wicked men, put him to death by nailing him to the cross.' Is Peter saying that God foresaw Calvary, or that God planned Calvary? Foreknowledge here obviously means foreordination. It can mean nothing else. Every prophecy in the Old Testament about Jesus proves this. The Old Testament prophecies were not speculative guesses, but revelations of what God had planned, as Acts 4:28 makes clear, 'They did what your power and will had decided beforehand should happen.'

Romans 8:29. 'For those God foreknew he also predestined to be conformed to the likeness of his Son.' In verse 28 Paul speaks of God's purpose for his people. The reason why all things work together for good is that the Christian's life is set in the context of God's eternal purpose. Therefore all that comes to us in life belongs to this great sovereign purpose of God. The apostle immediately goes on in verse 30 to speak of the purpose of God in terms of predestination, calling, justification and glorification, and in this context foreknowledge and predestination are not too different.

Romans 11:2. 'God did not reject his people, whom he foreknew.' Paul is dealing with the case of the Jews, God's chosen people. He is not saying that God will not reject Israel because he knows certain things about them, what they will do, or not do. There is no sense in that argument. Paul is saying that it is inconceivable that God, having chosen these people, will now forsake them. 'Foreknow' carries the meaning of 'choose'.

1 Peter 1:2,20. 'Chosen according to the foreknowledge of God the Father... He was chosen before the creation of the world.' The word translated 'foreknowledge' in verse 2 is translated in the Authorized Version as 'foreordained' in verse 20, and in the NIV as 'chosen'. Dr Lloyd-Jones says of this, 'The translators of the Authorized Version are at times inconsistent with themselves. In this statement in 1 Peter 1, they very rightly translated it as "foreordained", and they should have done the same everywhere else. They so translated there because it is obvious that it could not possibly mean anything else.'[3]

These uses of the word in the New Testament all underline the sovereignty of God in our salvation. Dr Lloyd-Jones sums up this usage: 'Foreknowledge carries the meaning of God setting His love upon, and ordaining and determining certain things for His people. Indeed there is very little difference between foreknowledge and predestination.'[4]

Finally, let us consider the words of Jesus when he said, 'I am the good shepherd; I know my sheep and my sheep know me... My sheep listen to my voice; I know them, and they follow me' (John 10:14,27). Here again 'know' means more than 'know about'. Because Jesus knows us he has set his love upon us with electing grace. He lays down his life for the sheep, he gives them eternal life and they can never perish. What a comfort this is! It is an encouragement to pray even in the most hopeless of situations, for the most unlikely of people to be saved. God is sovereign; therefore anything is possible.

'Were there no election,' says Dr Packer, 'there would be no calling, and no conversions, and all evangelistic activity would fail. But as it is, we know, as we spread God's truth, that his word will not return to him void. He has sent it to be the means whereby he calls His elect, and it will prosper in the thing for which He has sent it.'[5]

5.
The holiness of God

Holiness is the attribute of God which the Bible emphasizes more than any other. It is so crucial to the being of God that it is true to say it permeates every other attribute. Thus we can speak of God's holy love, his holy wrath, his holy providence, and so on. It is not surprising, therefore, that the Scriptures exhort us to address God as the Holy One.

> 'Exalt the Lord our God
>   and worship at his holy mountain,
>   for the Lord our God is holy'
>
> (Psalm 99:9).

> 'Holy and awesome is his name'
>
> (Psalm 111:9).

> 'Who will not fear you, O Lord,
>   and bring glory to your name?
> For you alone are holy'
>
> (Revelation 15:4).

In 1 Samuel 2:2 we are told, 'There is no one holy like the Lord.' There is no one so absolutely pure and free from all moral imperfections. The Puritan John Howe said, 'Holiness runs through the rest [of the attributes] and casts lustre upon them. It is an attribute of attributes.' Holiness means not only

an entire freedom from all moral evil, but also an absolute
moral perfection. Tozer explains it like this: 'Holy is the way
God is. To be holy he does not conform to a standard. He is that
standard. He is absolutely holy with an infinite,
incomprehensible fulness of purity that is incapable of being
other than it is. Because He is holy, all his attributes are holy;
that is, whatever we think of as belonging to God must be
thought of as holy.'[1]

As believers we need early in our Christian life to appreciate
something of the holiness of God. The unregenerate man or
woman and the nominal Christian do not believe in a holy God.
They have vague notions of a sentimental god who tolerates
sin. But the God and Father of the Lord Jesus Christ is not like
that. He is in a category of his own. There is none like him in
sovereignty and mercy, but particularly with regard to holiness.
God is holy with an absolute holiness that knows no degrees or
variableness and this holiness is peculiarly his.

How this affects us

God's sovereignty saves us and his providence keeps and
guides us, and we find great comfort in these truths. But his
holiness overwhelms us and fills us with awe. We find it
difficult to grasp holiness. The truth is that holiness is completely
outside of our experience. We may know what we consider to
be good men, or men who are wise, powerful and loving, but
where is the man who is absolutely holy? It is a concept beyond
our grasp and consequently God's holiness is something we
cannot even imagine.

An awareness of the holiness of God will affect how we
worship. Both Moses and Joshua were told to take off their
shoes because the ground on which they stood was holy
ground. It was holy because God was there. The hallmark of
biblical worship is not noise and flippant familiarity, but awe,

wonder, reverence and deep joy. It is the holy God that we worship and there is no worship without an awareness of the divine holiness. This is emphasized in the Old Testament structure of the tabernacle. God dwelt symbolically in the Holy of Holies and a thick veil separated the people from him. No one was allowed to enter the Holy of Holies except the high priest once a year on the Day of Atonement. When Christ died the veil was torn in two and this opened up access to the holy God, but it did not change the fact of the holiness of God. Worship is still a privilege of grace. Tozer defines worship as 'To feel in the heart a humbling but delightful sense of admiring awe and astonished wonder, and to express it in some appropriate manner. Worship is awesome wonder and overpowering love in the presence of God.'[2] It is impossible to worship like this without an awareness of the holiness of God.

This awareness will also affect how we live. To Israel first, then to all Christians, God says, 'Be holy, for I am holy.' He did not say that we are to be as holy as he is, for that would be to demand the absolute holiness that belongs to God alone. None the less there is a degree of holiness that God demands from his people. And the proof that we belong to God is that there is a measure of holiness in us. It is what the New Testament calls the fruit of the Spirit. Lack of this makes a real meeting with God a shattering experience, like the one Isaiah had in chapter 6 of his prophecy. It was not that the prophet was a terrible sinner; it was simply that in the presence of the holiness of God he felt so vile and unclean. The apostle John had a similar experience in Revelation 1. When he saw that amazing revelation of Christ John 'fell at his feet as though dead' (Revelation 1:13-17).

As we read these things it must make us wonder what we really know of meeting with God. Have we seen the holiness of God? Do we want to see it? Our sin and worldliness can make us afraid of really drawing near and we satisfy ourselves with much less of God than he wants us to have. But what do we do with our sin and lack of holiness? Tozer tells us what to do: 'We must hide our unholiness in the wounds of Christ as Moses hid himself in the cleft of the rock while the glory of God passed by. We must take refuge from God in God. Above all we must believe that God sees us perfect in his Son while he disciplines and chastens and purges us that we may be partakers of his holiness.'[3]

The law and the cross

As we understand more of God's holiness, we shall inevitably also understand more of man's sinfulness and the necessity of Christ's atoning death on the cross. This is because God's holiness is revealed primarily in the law and the cross.

God is holy and everything he does and instigates is holy. This is seen clearly in the law, which Romans 7:12 says is holy. The law forbids sin in all its forms, whether it be the vileness of idolatry, murder, or adultery, or sin in its more subtle forms of disobeying parents and covetousness. God forbids sin because it is repugnant to his holiness and it pollutes and harms his creation. If the law cannot restrict sin then God will destroy it. God's wrath and justice are direct consequences of his holiness. God hates sin as a mother hates the disease that is killing her child.

We mentioned earlier that the unregenerate do not believe in a holy God. This is because they will not take seriously their sin and its consequences. As Pink says, 'The fact is that nothing makes more manifest the terrible depravity of man's heart and his enmity against the living God than to have set before him One who is infinitely and immutably holy. His own idea of sin is practically limited to what the world calls "crime". Anything short of that man palliates as "defects", "mistake", "infirmities", etc. and even where sin is owned at all, excuses and extenuations are made for it.'[4]

The best the law can do is to restrain sin. It is the cross that defeats it; thus the cross is the greatest demonstration of God's holiness. While it is the love of God that makes the cross possible, it is the holiness of God that makes it necessary. God cannot and will not tolerate sin. Sin must be punished and from his holiness God's wrath flows to smite sin. Stephen Charnock wrote, 'Never did divine holiness appear more beautiful and lovely than at the time our Saviour's countenance was most marred in the midst of his dying groans.'[5] To satisfy his holiness God's love made Jesus a propitiation for our sin.

He bore the punishment our sin deserved. Jesus himself acknowledges this in Psalm 22. The answer to the question of verse 1, 'My God, my God, why have you forsaken me?' is to be found in verse 3. God is the Holy One.

'There will be several consequences for those who come to the knowledge of the Holy,' writes James Montgomery Boice. 'Firstly, they will learn to hate sin. We do not naturally hate sin. In fact, the opposite is true. We generally love sin and are loath to part with it. But we must learn to hate sin, or else we will learn to hate God who requires a holy life from those who are Christ's followers. We see a great tension during the lifetime of the Lord Jesus Christ. Some saw His holiness, came to hate sin and became his followers. Others saw him, same to hate him and eventually crucified him. Secondly, those who have come to the knowledge of the Holy One through faith in the Lord Jesus Christ will learn to love righteousness and strive for it. We cannot be holy in the same sense that God is holy. But we can be holy in the area of a righteous and upright walk before Him.'[6]

6.
The providence of God

By the providence of God we mean the unceasing activity of God working in the affairs of men and women. He upholds, guides and governs all events and circumstances, and providence is a direct consequence of divine sovereignty. God is King over all his creation, doing just what he wants. He 'works everything in conformity with the purposes of his will' (Ephesians 1:11). Throughout history there have been various views as to how the world is governed. For instance, Deism believed in a remote creator, a god who set the world in motion, but who now stands apart from it like a spectator. Other views see chance or fate as the governing factors. Over against these the Bible teaches that all history is under God's providence.

Examples of providence

The famine in Egypt appeared to men to be the result of natural causes, but Joseph said, 'The matter has been firmly decided by God' (Genesis 41:32). The *Heidelberg Catechism* defines providence as 'the almighty and ever-present power of God whereby he still upholds, as it were by his own hand, heaven and earth together with all creatures, and rules in such a way that leaves and grass, rain and drought, fruitful and unfruitful years, food and drink, health and sickness, riches and poverty, and everything else, come to us not by chance but by his fatherly hand.' The famine in Egypt is an example of this, and so too are the words of Jesus regarding sparrows in Matthew 10:29: 'Not one of them will fall to the ground apart from the will of your Father.' Nations and individuals are under the rule of providence: 'The Most High is sovereign over the kingdoms of men and gives them to anyone he wishes' (Daniel 4:17).

These are only a few examples from Scripture which show clearly the providence of God. It is not luck, nor chance, nor fate, but providence that governs the world. God's will is worked out in the lives of men and women, whether they are believers or not. It was no accident that brought Rebekah to the well to meet Abraham's servants (Genesis 24). Or consider Joseph's clear testimony to God's ordering affairs: 'Do not be distressed and do not be angry with yourselves for selling me here, because it was to save lives that God sent me ahead of you ... to preserve for you a remnant on earth and to save your lives by a great deliverance. So then, it was not you who sent me here, but God' (Genesis 45:4-8). It was not by chance that Pharaoh's daughter found the baby Moses, or that Esther became queen 'for such a time as this'. The Bible abounds in its examples of providence and sees God's ruling hand in all things.

Problems

Because providence is so akin to sovereignty it gives rise to the same problems in human minds that we saw in the case of sovereignty.

If God is good and God rules, why is the world in such a mess? Why is there so much wickedness, and why do the wicked seem to prosper? It is not difficult to sympathize with Asaph when he said,

'For I envied the arrogant
    when I saw the prosperity of the wicked.
They have no struggles;

their bodies are healthy and strong.
They are free from the burdens common to man;
 they are not plagued by human ills'

(Psalm 73:3-5).

Here was a righteous man trying to live a good life, but all the unfairness of life depressed him and he concluded, 'Surely in vain have I kept my heart pure; in vain have I washed my hands in innocence.' What is the answer to this dilemma? The psalmist gives it himself in verse 17 when he talks of the final destiny of the wicked. We are not to judge God's providential dealings simply in terms of what we see in this world. There is eternity to consider, and ultimately we will see how good is God's rule. There is much we cannot understand, but like Asaph we know that 'You guide me with your counsel, and afterwards you will take me into glory' (Psalm 73:24).

Inevitably the problem of man's responsibility and accountability arises in considering providence. 'The providence of God does not relieve us of responsibility. God works through means (the integrity, hard work, obedience and faithfulness of Christian people, for example). The providence of God does not relieve us of the need to make wise judgements or to be prudent. On the other hand, it does relieve us of anxiety in God's service. Rather than being a cause for self-indulgence, compromise, rebellion or any other sin, the doctrine of providence is actually a sure ground for trust and a spur to faithfulness.'[1]

There is no doubt that providence will confuse us on occasions. Thomas Watson, the Puritan, gives us good advice when this happens: 'God is to be trusted when his providences seem to run contrary to his promises. God promised David to give him the crown, to make him king; but providence turns contrary to his promise; David was pursued by Saul, was in danger of his life; but all this while it was David's duty to trust God. The Lord doth often times, by cross providence,

bring to pass his providence. God promised Paul the lives of all
that were with him in the ship; but now the providence of God
seems to run quite contrary to his promise; the winds blow, the
ship splits and breaks in pieces; and thus God fulfilled his
promise; upon the broken pieces of the ship, they all come safe
to shore. Trust God when providences seem to run quite
contrary to promises.'² Another Puritan, John Flavel, made the
wise observation that 'Some providences, like Hebrew letters,
must be read backwards.'

Jeremiah

Let us now seek to illustrate the providence of God in a
remarkable event in Jeremiah 32.

Jeremiah was in prison because he persisted in declaring
that God was going to judge Judah and deliver them to the
Babylonians. Zedekiah the king did not want to hear of God's
judgement and providence. He particularly did not like being
told, 'If you fight against the Babylonians, you will not
succeed' (v. 5). At this point the prophet was instructed by God
to buy a field which belonged to his cousin. He obeyed and the
legal transaction was meticulously carried out (vv. 11-12), but
in the circumstances the whole thing seemed so pointless. If the
enemy were going to capture the land what was the use of
buying a field? The point was that God said, 'Houses, fields
and vineyards will again be bought in this land' (v. 15).
Jeremiah was no doubt somewhat confused, but nevertheless
he trusted God and obeyed.

Having obeyed, he prays in verses 16-25. The prayer is
illuminating. Here is a man with a great view of the sovereignty
of God (vv. 17-19). He sees God moving nations in order to
bless his people (vv. 20-22). He sees God punishing this
blessed people because of their sin (v. 23). In fact, he sees God
at work in everything and it is all done for a purpose (v. 24). But

it is evident in verse 25 that he is still confused: 'The city is going to be lost, but you say buy the field and have the transaction witnessed.'

Now look at God's answer in verse 27. Here is a declaration of God's sovereignty. He controls the world. The rain falls and the sun shines at his command. Men live and move and breathe only because of God's grace. He is Lord and King and nothing is too hard or impossible for him. We need to be reminded of this. Jeremiah knew it and voiced it in verse 17: 'Nothing is too hard for you,' he said. Then God challenged him in verse 27: 'Do you really believe it? Is anything too hard for me?'

All too often our thoughts of God can be high and correct but only theoretical. Is our doctrine of the sovereignty of God a theory, or do we believe it? The providence of God brings us down to earth with a bump and takes divine sovereignty out of the realm of theological theory and reveals it to be completely realistic and practical. God is sovereign and does control (see v. 42). The whole business of buying the field was to show this (vv. 43-44). In a world of uncertainty and confusion, the doctrine of the providence of God should thrill the heart of the Christian. Even though at times circumstances may deny it. God is in control. We are not leaves blown around by the winds of chance and fate but the children of God held fast in providential hands.

> Great providence of heaven —
> What wonders shine
> In its profound display
> Of God's design;
> It guards the dust of earth,
> Commands the hosts above,
> Fulfils the mighty plan
> Of his great love.
>
> The kingdoms of this world
> Lie in its hand;

See how they rise or fall
At its command!
Through sorrow and distress
Tempestuous storms that rage
God's kingdom yet endures
From age to age.

Its darkness dense is but
A radiant light;
Its oft-perplexing ways
Are ordered right.
Soon all its winding paths
Will end, and then the tale
Of wonder shall be told
Beyond the veil.

(David Charles)

7.
The immutability of God

To say that God is immutable means that he never changes. He tells us himself in Malachi 3:6, 'I the Lord do not change.' James in his epistle wrote that our heavenly Father 'does not change like shifting shadows'. Even the name with which God reveals himself declares this truth in Exodus 3:14: 'I am who I am.' Dr Packer says of this title, 'This "name" is not a description of God, but simply a declaration of His self-existence, and His eternal changelessness; a reminder to mankind that He has life in Himself, and that what He is now, He is eternally.'[1]

Like many of the other attributes of God, immutability is alien to our experience. It shows us that God is totally different from us. Samuel the prophet declared that God is 'not a man, that he should change his mind' (1 Samuel 15:29). All our experience, both of ourselves and others, is of change. We grow old and change physically. Our understanding and beliefs change, and our mood can change from day to day. Sometimes the change is for the better, sometimes for the worse, but it is always change. Often we cannot cope with change and it causes great sorrow. For instance, a young couple get married. They are in love and pledge that love 'until death do us part'. Yet in a couple of years they are separated. Why? She says, 'He changed. He was not as kind and considerate as when we were courting.' He says, 'She changed. She is not as young and attractive as she was.' On the other hand, change can be for the

good. If man was not capable of change we could never be
converted and become Christians.

The problem is that we are so used to change that we tend
to forget that God never changes. Or if we do not forget it, we
ignore it.

God's nature

God's nature is such that he cannot change. As we have seen, all
change must be either for the better or the worse. As A. W. Pink
put it, 'He cannot change for the better, for he is already perfect;
and being perfect he cannot change for the worse.'[2] 'God is God.
He can be no less and no more than he is. He does not grow old.
He does not mature or develop. He does not gain new powers or
lose those he had. He is God and always the same. 'Created things
have a beginning and an ending, but not so their Creator. The
answer to the child's question. "Who made God?" is simply that
God did not need to be made, for he was always there.'[3]

Like God's holiness, his immutability touches all his other
attributes, so that God's power is inexhaustible, his love is
everlasting, his mercy endures for ever and, says Psalm 119,

> 'Your word ... is eternal,
>   It stands firm in the heavens.
> Your faithfulness continues through all generations.'

This is not empty theological speculation. All that God is he
has always been and will always be. Nothing about God needs
modifying. Nothing the Bible says about him will be rescinded.

This great truth has a bearing upon the life of every human
being. We are living in days when people do not believe in
absolutes. Everything now is relative. Morality is relative, so
that what was unacceptable twenty-five years ago (things like
homosexuality, nudity on beaches, foul language in public) is

now acceptable. Nothing is right or wrong in and of itself. Morality changes with the whim and fancy of the age. But the doctrine of divine immutability says this is wrong. God is unchanging, therefore his truth is unchanging and his requirements are unchanging. There is an absolute, unchanging truth and therefore what used to be wrong is still wrong. It is nothing to do with being modern or old-fashioned. It is all to do with the unchanging character of God. 'When we read our Bibles, therefore, we need to remember that God still stands to all the promises, and demands, and statements of purpose, and words of warning, that are there addressed to New Testament believers. These are not relics of a bygone age, but an eternally valid revelation of the mind of God towards his people in all generations, so long as this world lasts.'[4]

The effects of this

God's attitude to sin has never changed. He who said the wages of sin is death has not changed his mind. He who opened hell for sin has never closed its terrible doors. People who defy God and break his laws must not think everything is all right because the divine law is old. It may be old, but it is true and everlasting, and God has warned, 'Be sure your sin will find you out.' The immutability of God is an awesome reality for unrepentant sinners. But such people can also find hope in this truth. God's way of salvation never changes either, so there is still hope if they believe the gospel and repent of their sin.

To the backslidden Christian, the one who has grown cold in his love for God, the unchanging character of God says, 'God still loves you. His love is unchangeable. The love he had for you when you loved and served him has never wavered or diminished despite your sin. It cannot because it is immutable. Therefore if you come back to him you will be received gladly. It is your love that has changed, not God's.'

What a comfort this truth always brings to the Christian!
God is always the same. If he willed one thing today and
another tomorrow, we could never trust him. But his purpose
is fixed, his will stable and his truth sure. 'Here then is a rock
on which we may fix our feet, while the mighty torrent is
sweeping away everything around us. The permanence of
God's character guarantees the fulfilment of his promises.'[5]

What a difference the immutability of God makes to
prayer! If God was always changing prayer would be impossible.
We could never pray with confidence if we had a changeable
God. Such thoughts as, 'Will God hear me today?' 'Will he be
understanding?' 'Will he want to bother with me?' would
dominate our thinking and in effect destroy all boldness in
prayer. But the one we come to is always the same. God is
always open to our praises and groans, and he is always
sympathetic. So pray Christian, pray.

A right understanding of the immutability of God gives to
us a great and proper spirit of expectancy. The God who
opened the Red Sea, brought down fire on Carmel and turned
the world upside down through the preaching of the apostles is
the same God we love and serve. He has the same power and
the same desire to bless his people. There is no need for any
Christian to live in the past when we have an unchangeable
God.

8.
The omnipotence of God

John tells us that in heaven he heard the voice of a great multitude of the saints filling the courts of glory with a mighty thunderous proclamation: 'Alleluia: for the Lord God omnipotent reigneth' (Revelation 19:6, AV). This cry shows us the sovereignty of God. He is the Lord and he reigns supreme. But it also shows us another attribute of God that all Scripture delights in declaring. He is the Lord God omnipotent. 'Sovereignty and omnipotence must go together. One cannot exist without the other. To reign, God must have power, and to reign sovereignly, he must have all power. And that is what omnipotent means, having all power.'[1] When the word 'omnipotent' is used in the Bible it is only ever used about God. He alone is almighty.

Real power

The God of the Bible is a God of varied and limitless power and it is impossible to compare with this power the greatest achievements of the mightiest men. Have you ever stood in a great cathedral and admired the huge structure and vast arches? You may ask, who made this? When you look in the guidebook you see it took thousands of men over a hundred years to construct that building. Then go outside and look at the sky, the stars and the moon; see the glory of the mountains and the sea, and ask, who made all this? The answer is, God did and did it

alone and did it in a moment. He said, 'Let there be, ...' and
there was. That is the power of God. I remember in the 1950s
seeing the film *The Ten Commandments* and being particularly
impressed with the scene of the opening of the Red Sea. I
thought it was very clever; it looked so real. Then I suddenly
thought, God actually did it. No trick camera work, but
omnipotence parted those waters. That is real power.

The reality of God's power seems to confuse men. They do not
believe it and dismiss the miracles of the Bible as myth. It is
impossible, they say. But impossible to whom? To men, to
politicians, to scientists, yes, but not to God. We must not limit
God by our limitations. 'Before man can work he must have tools
and materials, but God began with nothing, and by his word alone
out of nothing made all things. The intellect cannot grasp it.'[2]

Another difficulty men have with divine omnipotence is that
they misinterpret it. You do not have to read the Bible for very
long to discover the difference in outlook between the men of
Scripture and modern man. We are suffering from what Tozer
called a secularized mentality. Where those men saw God, we see
the laws of nature. We have reduced the omnipotent God to a set
of laws and forget that what we see in nature is simply the paths
that God's power and wisdom take. As Tozer put it, 'Science
observes how the power of God operates, discovers a regular
pattern somewhere and fixes it as a "law". The uniformity of
God's activities in his creation enables the scientist to predict the
course of natural phenomena. The trustworthiness of God's
behaviour in his world is the foundation of all scientific truth.
Upon it the scientist rests his faith and from there he goes on to
achieve great and useful things in such fields as those of navigation,
chemistry, agriculture, and the medical arts.'[3]

A true perspective

As Christians we need to see beyond these impersonal laws to
the hand of God. God's power is real and omnipotence is a real

attribute of God. If we forget this we shall be in serious trouble. For too long we have allowed the world's secularized mentality to colour our views of God. Consequently the sovereign, omnipotent God of Scripture has become a helpless, feeble God, who can only do what we allow. We have emptied God of omnipotence and replaced it with sentiment.

This inevitably affects our views of Jesus. In modern Christianity Jesus is often a sad, pathetic figure standing out in the cold, begging to come in. This is typified in Holman Hunt's painting *The Light of the World*. But this is not the Jesus of Scripture, who walked on water, calmed the storm, raised the dead and commands all men everywhere to repent. Somehow or other we have lost sight of Jesus, mighty to save. We confess to the same faith and to believing the same doctrines as Spurgeon and Whitefield, but do we have any acquaintance at all with the almighty God whom they knew so intimately?

If God is sovereign then he must be omnipotent. Without all power, many of his other attributes would only be gestures. They depend for their effectiveness on his omnipotence. 'The power of God is that ability and strength whereby he can bring to pass whatsoever he pleases, whatsoever his infinite wisdom may direct, and whatsoever the infinite purity of his will may resolve... As holiness is the beauty of all God's attributes, so power is that which gives life and action to all the perfections of the divine nature. How vain would be the eternal counsels, if power did not step in to execute them. Without power his mercy would be but feeble pity, his promises an empty sound, his threatenings a mere scarecrow. God's power is like himself; infinite, eternal, incomprehensible; it can neither be checked, restrained, nor frustrated by the creature.'[4]

Encouragement

The power of God works *for* his people and *through* his people. Tozer wrote, 'The church began in power, moved in power and

moved just as long as she had power. When she no longer had power she dug in for safety and sought to conserve her gains. But her blessings were like manna; when they tried to keep it over night it bred worms and stank... In church history every return to New Testament power has marked a new advance somewhere, a fresh proclamation of the Gospel, an upsurge of missionary zeal; and every diminution of power has seen the rise of some new mechanism for conservation and defence.'[5]
These words of Tozer bring us a serious warning but also great encouragement. The Christian church at the end of the twentieth century seems so weak and powerless, and this discourages Christians in their attempts to serve the Lord. Our lack of power puts us on the defensive, but that must be wrong. An awareness of powerlessness ought to turn us in desperation to the omnipotent God who, time and time again, has worked in power in his church. This does not mean that we do nothing until God comes in power, but it encourages us to trust God as we seek to serve him.

Spurgeon advises us, 'And now as to thy service, to which thou art called by the Lord. If he be so strong, do not think of thine own weakness any longer, except as being a platform for his strength. Hast thou only one talent? God's Holy Spirit is not limited in power. He can make thine one talent as fruitful as another man's ten. Art thou weak as water? Then rejoice this day, and glory in infirmity, because the power of God shall rest upon thee. Think not of what thou canst do — that is a very small affair, but consider what he can do by thee. He can strengthen the feeble against the strong.'[6]

Tozer gives a lovely example: 'The Presbyterian pastor A. B. Simpson, approaching middle age, broken in health, deeply despondent and ready to quit the ministry, chanced to hear the simple Negro spiritual:

Nothing is too hard for Jesus,
No man can work like him.

'Its message sped like an arrow to his heart, carrying faith and hope and life for body and soul. He sought a place of retirement and after a season alone with God arose to his feet, completely cured, and went forth in fulness of joy and founded what has since become one of the largest foreign missionary societies in the world. For thirty-five years after this encounter with God, he laboured prodigiously in the service of Christ. His faith in the God of limitless power gave him all the strength he needed to carry on.'[7]

9.
The wisdom of God

Wisdom is far more than just an accumulation of knowledge. Wisdom is using knowledge for the highest and best ends. A man may have vast knowledge from many years of study and still lack wisdom in his use of that knowledge. Dr Packer defines wisdom as 'the power to see, and the inclination to choose, the best and highest goal, together with the surest means of attaining it.'[1] This we find in God. He is, as Paul tells us, God only wise. Clearly God has all knowledge, but more than that, he is wise. What he knows he uses for good. In our God there is the awe-inspiring combination of wisdom and power. 'Wisdom and power are his' (Daniel 2:20). 'His wisdom is profound, his power is vast' (Job 9:4). This combination is important because it means that when God's wisdom seeks to do good it is never frustrated by lack of power to achieve its aim. Once again we see how all God's attributes hang together and feed and strengthen each other.

Wisdom working

Wisdom is the ability to devise perfect ends and to achieve those ends by the most perfect means. Divine wisdom sees the end from the beginning, so there is no need to guess or calculate. Because of this all God's work is done in perfect wisdom and nothing he does could be done better.

This must encourage us greatly. What use is a god who is

wise but has no power to carry out his wise decrees? What use is a god of little wisdom who always has to guess, to readjust and to estimate? What use is a god who is only wise after the event? Our God is not like that. Everything he does is right first time. Such a God can be trusted without any reservations. Tozer warns us, 'It is vitally important that we hold the truth of God's infinite wisdom as a tenet of our creed; but this is not enough. We must by the exercise of faith and by prayer bring it into the practical world of our day-by-day experience. To believe actively that our heavenly Father constantly spreads around us providential circumstances that work for our present good and our everlasting well-being brings to the soul a veritable benediction. Most of us go through life praying a little, planning a little, jockeying for position, hoping but never being quite certain of anything, and always secretly afraid that we will miss the way. This is a tragic waste of truth and never gives rest to the heart.'[2]

Providence would be a terrifying thought if God were not wise. But the knowledge of his wisdom encourages us to rest in his providence.

> Leave to his sovereign sway
> To choose and to command;
> So shalt thou wondering own his way,
> How wise, how strong his hand.
> Far, far above thy thought
> His counsel shall appear,
> When fully he the work hath wrought
> That caused thy needless fear.
>
> (Paul Gerhardt)

Trusting God's wisdom

There are times, particularly in troubles and sorrow, when we are tempted to think God has made a mistake. But time always proves the wisdom of God. He was right, and he always is.

How much pain we should spare ourselves if we remembered this! We may be baffled at things which happen to us, but God knows exactly what he is doing. If we believe this we ought not to hesitate to trust his wisdom even when he leaves us in the dark as to the purpose of events.

This is not the same as fatalism. We are not to allow circumstances to walk all over us and wipe their feet on us like a doormat. Trusting God's wisdom does not mean that we relinquish the use of the God-given facility to think. Sometimes God's wisdom is worked out as we use God's means and methods. Take, for instance, the apostle Paul. In various incidents when he faced adverse circumstances, we see that he did not just passively accept them as God's providential wisdom for him. He acted differently in each situation, sometimes accepting the difficulty and at other times avoiding it.

Acts 14:5-6: He fled from the difficulty.
Acts 21:10-16: He accepted the difficulty.
Acts 23:12-34: He used the authorities to avoid the difficulty.

When Paul fled or used the authorities, he was not refusing to accept the providence and wisdom of God, but rather refusing to bow down to the sinful and evil plans of men. We should do the same in similar situations, but there are times when we can do nothing. Then we must believe in the wisdom of God and trust him.

Recognizing God's wisdom

If you had the power to plan completely your life and circumstances, what would you do? Most of us would plan for good health, happiness and enough money to remove all worries. But would these things of necessity enhance and deepen our relationship with God, or promote our spiritual growth? Do not forget that Jacob was of no real use to God until God had lamed him. Tricky, crafty Jacob planned and schemed his way through life and he prospered for twenty years as God let him have his own way. Then at Peniel God put his thigh joint out as a continual reminder in his body of his own spiritual weakness. For the rest of his life his limp reminded him of how much he needed God, and Jacob was a different man after Peniel. That is the wisdom of God. His ways are not our ways, but they are always for our good.

We should not be too taken aback when unexpected and unsettling things happen to us. Do not ask in self-pity, 'Why?' Ask rather, in the light of God's wisdom, 'What is God trying to teach me in this experience?' And praise him that he cares enough to try to teach you. 'Perhaps,' as Packer suggests, 'he means to strengthen us in patience, good humour, compassion, humility, or meekness, by giving us some extra practice in exercising these graces under specially difficult conditions. Perhaps he has new lessons in self-denial and self-trust to teach us. Perhaps he wishes to break us of complacency, or unreality or undetected forms of pride and conceit... Or perhaps God is preparing us for forms of service of which at present we have no inkling.'[3]

Do you remember Paul's thorn in the flesh in 1 Corinthians 12? What was the purpose of this? Why did God allow it? Paul knew: 'To keep me from becoming conceited because of these surpassingly great revelations, there was given me a thorn in my flesh.' Three times he asked God to remove it, but God would not. Instead Paul was told, 'My grace is sufficient for you, for my power is made perfect in weakness.' The reaction of the apostle to this was not to complain of God's action but to rejoice. Here was a man who saw the wisdom of God and knew that it would always work for his good.

The human mind is so blinded by sin that it can rarely at first glance recognize God's wisdom. There is no greater demonstration of this than in the ministry of Christ himself. When God sought finally to break the power of Satan in the world he sent a baby. How foolish, to our understanding! But 1 Corinthians 1:24 tells us that Christ is the wisdom and power of God. The so-called wisdom of this world cannot see this. 'Where is the wise man? Where is the scholar? Where is the philosopher of this age? Has not God made foolish the wisdom of the world? For since in the wisdom of God the world through its wisdom did not know him, God was pleased through the foolishness of what was preached to save those who believe. Jews demand miraculous signs and Greeks look for wisdom, but we preach Christ crucified; a stumbling-block to Jews and foolishness to Gentiles, but to those whom God has called, both Jews and Greeks, Christ the power of God and the wisdom of God. For the foolishness of God is wiser than man's wisdom, and the weakness of God is stronger than man's strength' (1 Corinthians 1:20-25).

Even the cross itself is foolishness to men. To the world it seems a complete failure, but here is the supreme wisdom of God. 'Christ Jesus ... has become for us wisdom from God — that is, our righteousness, holiness and redemption' (1 Corinthians 1:30).

If as believers we have been led to glory in the cross, and to see in it the wisdom of God to save us when we were in a lost and hopeless situation, surely we can also glory in the same wisdom acting in our lives even when we cannot understand what is happening. God knows what he is doing, so praise him that it is his wisdom, and not yours, that directs your life.

10.
The goodness of God

We have seen that the attributes of God reveal him to be totally different from man. He is sovereign and holy, immutable and omnipotent, and these things are true of no one but God alone. As we consider the goodness of God we may be tempted to think we know something of this. Whereas we know no one who is sovereign or omnipotent, we know many people who are good. The temptation, then, is to think of God's goodness as merely an extension of man's goodness. To do so would be very wrong. The Bible tells us, 'There is no one who does good, not even one' (Psalm 14, quoted in Romans 3:12). Jesus said the same thing to the rich young ruler: 'There is none good except God.'

God's goodness, like all his other attributes, is unique. Any goodness seen in man is only a reflection of that essential and unique goodness that is in God. Men are only good when they act and think as God would have them act and think. 'He is originally good, good of himself, which nothing else is; for all creatures are good only by participation and communication from God. He is essentially good; not only good, but goodness itself; the creature's good is a super-added quality, in God it is his essence. He is infinitely good; the creature's good is but a drop, but in God there is an infinite ocean or gathering together of good. He is eternally and immutably good, for he cannot be less good than he is; as there can be no addition made to him, so no subtraction from him.'[1]

Abundant in goodness

When we say that God is good, we are not thinking so much of his moral qualities, such as holiness and righteousness. We are referring more to his kindness, benevolence and generosity. God is tender-hearted and of quick sympathy. There is nothing harsh or unreasonable about him and his goodness is abundant in its generosity. But God's goodness is not weakness or softness. He is not some comfortable Santa Claus. Paul in Romans 11:22 speaks of the kindness and sternness of God and in our next chapter we shall see the wrath of God. God is not some soft touch that people can take advantage of and manipulate.

Having said that, we can praise God that by nature he is inclined to bestow blessings and he takes a holy pleasure in the happiness of his people. Thus the psalmist declares that God is good and does good. The goodness of God is the drive and motive behind all the blessings he daily bestows upon us. 'God created us,' said Tozer, 'because he felt good in his heart and he redeemed us for the same reason.'[2]

There is about God's goodness an infinite generosity, and without this we would be not only poorer but hopeless. He is 'the Lord, the Lord, the compassionate and gracious God, slow to anger, abounding in love and faithfulness, maintaining love to thousands, and forgiving wickedness, rebellion and sin' (Exodus 34:6-7). This revelation of God was the fulfilment of his promise in Exodus 33:19 that he would cause all his goodness to pass in front of Moses. Dr Packer says of these verses, 'All the particular perfections that are mentioned here, and all that go with them — God's truthfulness and trustworthiness, His unfailing justice and wisdom, His tenderness, forbearance, and entire adequacy to all who penitently seek His help, His noble kindness in offering men the exalted destiny of fellowship with Him in holiness and love — these things together make up God's goodness, in the

overall sense of the sum total of his revealed excellences.'[3]
Goodness seems such an ordinary word to use for all this, but
that is because we today have emptied the word of its unique
glory. To us goodness seems so normal, but it is not, as Psalm
14 and Romans 3 remind us.

The goodness of God is not some little thing, but of crucial
importance to us all. Every human being is completely
dependent upon this goodness for the means of life because
every material necessity comes from God. Every morsel of
food, every drop of water proclaims the fact that God is good.
We acknowledge this when we say grace before a meal and it
is right that we do this because it is easy to become complacent
and take God's goodness for granted. The unbeliever is always
doing this. He praises hard work, sweat and toil, fertilizers and
combine harvesters; these are the things he thanks for his food.
I remember as a teenager saying grace before a meal in the
factory canteen and being rebuked by a workmate. His argument
was that there was no need for me to thank God because I had
worked hard to earn the money to buy the food. As Christians
we recognize the necessity for work and effort, but above all
that we see the goodness of God. We agree completely with
David when he says,

> 'The Lord is good to all;
>> he has compassion on all he has made...
> The eyes of all look to you,
>> and you give them their food at the proper time.
> You open your hand
>> and satisfy the desires of every living thing'
>> (Psalm 145: 9,15-16).

Common grace

'The Lord is good to all,' refers to the common grace of God
whereby, as Jesus said, 'He causes his sun to rise on the evil and

the good, and sends rain on the righteous and the unrighteous' (Matthew 5:45). The psalmist is correct when he says the earth is full of God's goodness. The goodness of God is not some vague, nebulous thing, hidden away only to be revealed on special occasions. The earth is full of it. Every apple, every slice of bread, every breath we breathe testifies that God is good to all.

God's goodness does not just supply our needs, but it also provides pleasure in the necessities of life. We read of spacemen's food being compressed into little tablets. This is no doubt very clever and necessary in the circumstances, but can you imagine life like that? Brown tablets instead of roast beef, green ones instead of vegetables and gold ones instead of chips! What a good thing that we have a good God to feed us and not a group of scientists! Divine goodness is seen in the taste and flavour he gives to our food. God did not have to do this, but he wants us to enjoy his gifts.

The same is true with the world we live in. It is not merely functional but gloriously beautiful. The hues of green and blue, the fragrance of flowers and the singing of birds are all due to the goodness of God and this he does for all men and women, not only for those who love him. His enemies, even those who deny that he exists, can all enjoy the benefits of common grace. How great is the goodness of our God! Psalm 107, says Dr Packer, 'is a majestic panorama of the operations of divine goodness, transforming human lives.'[4] Four times the psalmist shouts out that men should thank God for his goodness and unfailing love. If the world does not do this, Christians should. ✻ We need to remind men of how indebted they are to the common grace of God. We can do this in several ways. One is saying grace before meals. Another is to acknowledge the goodness of God when people talk of luck or chance. Also we testify to the world by a willingness to accept God's ways. If we are always complaining and grumbling, what sort of testimony is that to the goodness of God? Yet another opportunity arises when men blame our good God for the many starving people in the world. We should be quick to point out how much good food is destroyed by men because it is not economic to distribute it. Is not this gross misuse of the world's natural resources one of the ways in which men show contempt for the riches of God's kindness? (Romans 2:4).

Saving grace

Of all people, the Christian has more cause than any to praise God for his goodness. It is God's goodness that led us to repentance (Romans 2:4). As well as common grace we have the saving grace of God for which to thank him. What greater good could we know than peace with God and sins forgiven? God is good to all men in some ways, but he is good to his people in all ways. There is nothing that God does for us that will not eventually result in our good. There may be times and experiences when we doubt this, but even then all things will work together for good because of the goodness of our God.

We shall let Charles Spurgeon have the last word on this: 'When others behave badly to us, it should only stir us up the more heartily to give thanks unto the Lord, because he is good; and when we ourselves are conscious that we are far from being good, we should only the more reverently bless him that he is good. We must never tolerate an instant's unbelief as to the goodness of the Lord; whatever else may be questioned, this is absolutely certain that Jehovah is good; his dispensations may vary, but his nature is always the same.'[5]

11.
The wrath of God

One of the values of studying the attributes of God is that we are able to see the whole biblical picture. All his attributes hang together and they affect each other. If we have properly understood the holiness of God we should see that divine wrath against sin is inevitable. Wrath is a product of holiness in the same way as indifference to sin is a product of godlessness. 'The wrath of God is his eternal detestation of all unrighteousness. It is the displeasure and indignation of divine equity against evil. It is the holiness of God stirred into activity against sin.'[1]

The Bible is not embarrassed to mention God's wrath. In fact there are more references in Scripture to the anger and wrath of God than there are to his love. In spite of this, today the subject is carefully avoided and even ridiculed. Packer writes, 'The modern habit throughout the Christian church is to play this subject down. Those who still believe in the wrath of God (not all do) say little about it; perhaps they do not think much about it. To an age which has unashamedly sold itself to the gods of greed, pride, sex, and self-will, the Church mumbles on about God's kindness, but says virtually nothing about His judgement... The fact is that the subject of divine wrath has become taboo in modern society, and Christians by and large have accepted the taboo and conditioned themselves never to raise the matter.'[2]

To ignore this is the height of foolishness. If divine wrath

is real then pretending it is not will not change anything. For
obvious reasons the subject is not popular, but it has to be
faced. God, who is utterly and completely holy, cannot regard
good and evil as the same. He cannot smile with the same
benevolence upon lies as upon truth. His holiness and justice
demand that he deals with sin; therefore they make hell as
inevitable for the lost as divine love makes heaven inevitable
for the saved.

There are probably two reasons why we have trouble with
the concept of the wrath of God. The first is that we are not holy
and therefore our attitudes to sin and evil are inconsistent.
Sometimes we applaud sin and at other times we criticize it.
The modern man, for instance, is broad-minded with regard to
adultery until his wife runs off with another man; then he
bitterly condemns it. But God is always consistent and always
hates sin. As far as God is concerned no sin is excusable, but,
in the mercy of God, all sin is pardonable in the Lord Jesus
Christ. The second problem is that we equate God's wrath with
man's wrath. But God's wrath is not vindictive nor an action
of uncontrolled temper. It is always a righteous reaction
against sin. It is always fair, always justified and never out of
control. There are no miscarriages of justice when God deals
with sin.

Wrath and justice

If we have any understanding of how holy God is and of how
sinful we are, a major problem will immediately confront us.
How can a guilty sinner ever be acceptable to a holy God? Even
the most shallow understanding of justice will show how
impossible this is. Modern theology answers the problem by
concocting a weak, sentimental god who is not bothered too
much with sin and welcomes everyone into heaven, including
atheists or agnostics. But the God and Father of our Lord Jesus

Christ is not weak and tolerant of sin, so the problem will not go away.

How can a sinner be right with God? John Murray says, 'The answer, of course, is that we cannot be right with him; we are all wrong with him. And we are all wrong with him because we all have sinned and come short of the glory of God. Far too frequently we fail to entertain the gravity of this fact. Hence the reality of our sin and the reality of the wrath of God upon us for our sin do not come into our reckoning.'[3] If we take God seriously, we must take sin seriously; this in turn will cause us to take justice and wrath seriously. Even God's love cannot bypass justice. So justice for guilty sinners seems inevitably to leave us with wrath and punishment. As we have seen, the Bible is very strong in asserting the reality of this wrath. Because the whole world is held accountable or guilty before God (Romans 3:19), we are all 'by nature objects of wrath' (Ephesians 2:3).

It is significant that when the Bible speaks of the wrath of God it often does so in legal or judicial terms, such as judge, law, verdict, guilt and condemnation. So 'the day of God's wrath,' says Paul in Romans 2:5, is the day 'when his righteous judgement will be revealed'.

Wrath and hell

'If you believe in wrath you must believe in eternal destruction. The parallels are used everywhere in the Scripture. There is nothing in the Scripture about another chance, another hope, another opportunity beyond death. There is nothing about "conditional mortality". It is "everlasting destruction from the presence of the Lord". People have tried to say that you can get over this by means of varying translations. You cannot; the terms are parallel everywhere, and the whole sense and meaning of the Scripture makes it quite plain and unmistakable. It is everlasting. And God's wrath against sin reveals and manifests itself as death, not only physical death, but still more terrible, spiritual death.'⁴

The one who controls hell is not Satan but God. Jesus tells us very plainly in Matthew 25:41 that hell is prepared *for* the devil and his disciples, not *by* the devil.

The Bible uses picture language to describe hell, but what is clear is that the fires of hell depict the wrath of the holy God. It is the awfulness of sin that makes hell necessary, but it is the holiness of God that creates hell. Hell is to be exposed, without a Saviour, to the holiness of God for all eternity (see 2 Thessalonians 1:6-9; Hebrews 10:27-31). In the New Testament it is Jesus who speaks mostly about hell and he has some terrible things to say about it, but by far the most terrible word that the Saviour uses about hell is 'eternal'. Hell is as eternal as heaven. There is no end to it. In life, even in the darkest moments, there is always the hope that things will get better. There is no such hope in hell. Souls are lost for ever. Charles Spurgeon said, 'On every chain in hell is written — for ever. If I could tell you that one day the fires of hell will burn out and that the lost might be saved, then there would be rejoicing in hell at the very thought — but it cannot be so; for ever damned, for ever cast into outer darkness.'

A present wrath

In Romans 1:18-32 Paul deals with God's wrath as it is experienced at the present time, not in a future hell. 'The wrath of God is being revealed' — it is a present reality for people who are godless and wicked. Paul explains who these people are. They suppress the truth of God and refuse the clear revelation of God to them. This inevitably leads to the terrible situation described in verses 21-23: 'For although they knew God, they neither glorified him as God nor gave thanks to him, but their thinking became futile and their foolish hearts were darkened. Although they claimed to be wise, they became fools and exchanged the glory of the immortal God for images made to look like mortal man and birds and animals and reptiles.'

To these people comes the wrath of God. It did not come, as it did upon Sodom and Gomorrah, in fire and brimstone. Nor did it come as it did to the world of Noah's day in a massive flood. God's wrath comes now in a more terrible way than these. In verses 24, 26 and 28 we are told that 'God gave them over' to their sin and its consequences. It is as if God says, 'If that is how you want to live, do it.'

As we look at society today we see rampant the very things mentioned in Romans 1. Man is wise enough to put himself on the moon, yet foolish enough for all the strife and killings that fill our newspapers (vv. 21-22). There is an abuse of God today whereby we make God and Jesus the subjects of blasphemous entertainment (v. 23). We see today aggressive lesbianism and homosexuality as blatant as that of Sodom and Gomorrah (vv. 26-27). We do not wish to retain the knowledge of God, and in recent years laws have been passed in Britain to legalize the things that God detests — homosexuality, divorce and abortion.

The wrath of God is very real and Christians need to take this seriously and plead with God for the souls of men and women.

12.
The love of God

The love of God is probably the most misunderstood of all the divine attributes. One of the main reasons for this is that people isolate John's famous statement in 1 John 4:8, 'God is love,' from everything else the Bible says about God. 'The apostle John, by the Spirit, wrote, "God is love," and some have taken his words to be a definite statement concerning the essential nature of God. This is a great error. John was by those words stating a fact, but he was not offering a definition,' says Tozer.[1] Many argue, if God is love, then love is God. Where we see love we see God; therefore we do not need Jesus nor the Bible nor the church. All that matters is love.

It may sound good to elevate love like this, but in fact it is disastrous if we truly want to know God. In 1 John 1:5 the apostle says that God is light, which is a reference to his holiness. That is just as strong and significant a statement as 'God is love.' One is as true and as important as the other. We have seen several times that we cannot isolate one attribute from the others. Each colours and affects the others, and in this love is no exception. When John says God is love, who is the God to whom he is referring? He is speaking of the God who created the world and then judged it with the flood; the God who in love and mercy called Abraham from idolatry and blessed him so abundantly, and who at the same time destroyed Sodom and Gomorrah; the God who so loved the world and yet just before John wrote his epistle destroyed Jerusalem in

A.D.70, using the Roman legions of Titus. This is John's God.
This is the God of the prophets, apostles and martyrs. This is
the God of the Lord Jesus Christ. To know this God properly
we must see him as he has chosen to reveal himself in
Scripture. If we isolate God's love from his other attributes we
shall inevitably reduce it to a sort of good-natured indulgence,
an amicable weakness, which empties it of its full biblical
glory. So what really is the love of God?

God's love is holy

God's love is kind, but it is also stern. 'God's love is stern, for it
expresses holiness in the lover and seeks holiness for the beloved.
Scripture does not allow us to suppose that because God is love
we may look to Him to confer happiness on people who will not
seek holiness, or to shield His loved ones from trouble when He
knows that they need trouble to further their sanctification.'[2] His
is a holy love that hates sin. Nowhere is this stated more clearly
than in John 3:16: 'For God so loved the world that he gave his
one and only Son, that whoever believes in him shall not perish
but have eternal life.' God loved a world that was perishing. Why
was it perishing? Because of God's judgement upon its sin. God
loved it in spite of its sin, but he did not ignore that sin; he sent
Jesus to die for man's sin and guilt.

God's love is sovereign

God's love is not influenced by anything outside itself. A. W.
Pink says, 'There was nothing whatever in the objects of his
love to call it into exercise, nothing in the creature to attract or
prompt it. The love which one creature has for another is
because of something in the object; but the love of God is free,
spontaneous, uncaused. The only reason why God loves is
found in his own sovereign will.'[3]

The love we have for each other is because of something in us that attracts each other. So we talk of love being blind, or we say sometimes, 'I do not know what she sees in him; if she really knew him she could never love him.' God's love is not blind. He knows us through and through. There is nothing in us to attract him, but he loves us because of this sovereign love which is free and spontaneous.

John spells out clearly this aspect of God's love in two great statements in his first epistle: 'This is love: not that we loved God, but that he loved us and sent his Son as an atoning sacrifice for our sins... We love because he first loved us' (1 John 4:10,19). If God had to wait for us to love him in order for him to love us, we should never be saved. Not only was there nothing in us to attract him, there was everything to repel him. Think of your sin and wickedness, yet God loves you. Praise him for a love which is sovereign.

God's love is eternal

As God is eternal, without beginning and without end, so too his love is eternal. 'I have loved you with an everlasting love' (Jeremiah 31:3). This is thrilling and it means that before we drew our first breath God loved us. Here is something in which we can greatly rejoice, because it means that if God's love had no beginning, it can have no ending. If God's love rested upon me in spite of my actions and character, then my actions and character will not drive it away. This is not a licence to sin but exactly the opposite; it is a great incentive to righteous living to thank and adore God for such a love.

God's love is indestructible

God's love is not a fragile, frail thing. God's love for us never wavers and nothing puts it under pressure. There is never a

moment when there is the slightest danger that this love will
cease. Simon Peter is a great example of this. Like us, he was
loved by God before the world began, but also like us, he only
became aware of this when he was saved. At Cæsarea Philippi
he had two contrasting experiences (read Matthew 16:13-23).
Peter earns first the great praise of Jesus and then the terrible
rebuke: 'Get behind me, Satan! You are a stumbling-block to
me; you do not have in mind the things of God, but the things
of men.' The point to remember is that, in both the praise and
the rebuke, God still loves Peter. Even when he falls, he is not
rejected as a failure, but loved and kept.

This does not mean that God takes pleasure in our sins. Sin
always grieves him, but he still loves us. Nothing destroys that.
But remember, whom he loves he chastens! The rebukes of
God, as well as his praises, are tokens of his love.

> 'Love is as strong as death...
> Many waters cannot quench love;
>   rivers cannot wash it away'
>
>   (Song of Songs 8:6-7).

God's love is immense

It is love without a limit. The hymn-writer speaks of the 'deep
love of Jesus, vast, unmeasured, boundless, free'. It reaches
down to us in the depths of sin, where we were slaves in
bondage, and sets us free. It gives Jesus to die on the cross as
our propitiation. Thus it satisfies the legal requirements of
divine wrath. Without this act of propitiation we could never
have been saved because the wrath of God would still be upon
us. On the cross that wrath fell on our substitute, the Lord Jesus
Christ.

If as Christians we are ever tempted to doubt God's love,
just go back to the cross. The crown of thorns tells us that God

loves us. The nail-prints spell out divine love. The broken body and shed blood proclaim to the world that God loves his people. How much does he love us? Enough to give his own Son to die for us. This is an immense love. And remember this love comes to you as an individual. Paul says, 'The Son of God ... loved me and gave himself for me' (Galatians 2:20). Tozer says of God's love, 'It is a personal, intimate thing too. God does not love populations; he loves people. He loves not masses, but men. He loves us all with a mighty love that has no beginning and can have no end.'[4]

The love of God is thrilling, breathtaking, but also challenging. It brings a serious challenge to every Christian, as Dr Packer points out: 'Is it true that God is love to me as a Christian? And does the love of God mean all that has been said? If so, certain questions arise.

'Why do I ever grumble and show discontent and resentment at the circumstances in which God has placed me?

'Why am I ever distrustful, fearful, or depressed?

'Why do I ever allow myself to grow cool, formal, and half-hearted in the service of the God who loves me so?

'Why do I ever allow my loyalties to be divided, so that God has not all my heart?

'John wrote that "God is love" in order to make an ethical point, "If God so loved us, we also ought to love one another" (1 John 4:11). Could an observer learn from the quality and degree of love that I show to others — my wife? my husband? my family? my neighbours? people at church? people at work? — anything at all about the greatness of God's love to me?

'Meditate upon these things. Examine yourself.'[5]

13.
The grace of God

Grace is the free, unmerited gift of God to a people who not only do not deserve it, but who deserve the opposite. It is God showing goodness to a people who deserve judgement, and as such it is one of the great foundation-stones of the gospel. The message of salvation through the Lord Jesus Christ is called in the New Testament 'the gospel of God's grace' (Acts 20:24). Without grace there is no gospel and the other attributes of God would be of only academic interest to us. It is grace that opens the door for us to know and enjoy God in all his fulness.

Grace and the modern man

It is impossible to stress too much the importance of grace, especially as modern man understands so little about it. Several years ago, when in some strange way John Newton's lovely hymn 'Amazing Grace' became a pop song and was top of the charts, it was played on a TV pop show and accompanied with a video of a gymnast on the parallel bars. This was grace! The whole concept of divine grace is foreign to the natural mind. Packer writes, 'Modern man is convinced that, despite all his little peccadilloes — drinking, gambling, reckless driving, "fiddling", back and white lies, sharp practice in trading, dirty reading, and what have you — he is at heart a thoroughly good fellow. Then, as pagans do (and modern man's heart is pagan

—make no mistake about that), he imagines God as a magnified image of himself, and assumes that God shares his own complacency about himself. The thought of himself as a creature fallen from God's image, a rebel against God's rule, guilty and unclean in God's sight, fit only for God's condemnation, never enters his head.'[1]

This arises because man has no understanding of the sovereignty and holiness of God, and he lives in a spiritual and moral fairyland. Reality is ignored and man loves to be told how good and generous he is. True, a great deal of money is raised from time to time for charity, but even so the human sin that makes so much of the charity necessary is usually ignored.

Modern man does not believe in punishment for wrongdoing. We have abolished capital punishment, schools are not allowed to discipline badly behaved children and we are told it is wrong for parents to smack their children. It is taken for granted that God feels the same way. We do not deserve punishment; therefore any concept of grace is unnecessary. Grace has become redundant. There will be no such thing as 'Amazing grace that saves a wretch like me,' if I do not believe I am a wretch. You will never delight in, 'Who is a pardoning God like thee, or who has grace so rich and free?' if you do not believe God punishes sin.

But once let a man become convinced of the truth that he is a sinner under the wrath and judgement of God, then grace will sweep him off his feet with wonder and joy, for it tells him how his Judge has become his Saviour. This is why, 'To the New Testament writers, grace is a wonder. Their sense of man's corruption and demerit before God, and of the reality and justice of his wrath against sin, is so strong that they find it simply staggering that there should be such a thing as grace at all — let alone grace that was so costly to God as the grace of Calvary.'[2]

Grace and salvation

Grace and salvation belong together like cause and effect. Paul says in Ephesians 2:5, 'It is by grace you have been saved,' and again in Titus 2:11, 'For the grace of God that brings salvation has appeared to all men.' The gospel centres on justification by faith and it is this that deals with our guilt. In justification peace with God is restored and access into his presence provided. In justification all the benefits of the gospel come to us, and we 'are justified freely by his grace' (Romans 3:24). Faith is the channel by which justification comes to us, but without grace faith would only be wishful thinking.

We may be tempted to think that there is little difference between love and grace. That would be wrong. There are two basic differences. Firstly, God's love plans salvation but God's grace provides it. Grace brings to us what the love of God wants us to have. Secondly, whereas God's love touches all men and women, because God so loved the world, God's grace is directed only towards the elect. In the Scriptures grace is never mentioned in connection with mankind generally, but only in reference to God's chosen people. The rich young ruler was loved by Jesus but remained unsaved, but if a man knows the grace of God he is saved.

Grace is necessary because without it sinful man has no hope, and grace is possible because of the loving and merciful character of God. The moment you see this, grace becomes the most thrilling thing there is. As you turn the pages of the Bible you see that the only explanation for the people we read about there is grace. Abraham the idolater becomes the friend of God. David, with all his waywardness, is a man after God's own heart. How are these things possible? How could a man like Saul of Tarsus, who so hated and despised Jesus, ever become the great apostle of the faith? He himself tells us how the most unlikely and ungodly of people become Christians: 'Do you not know that the wicked will not inherit the kingdom of God? Do not be deceived: Neither the sexually immoral nor idolaters nor adulterers nor male prostitutes nor homosexual offenders nor thieves nor the greedy nor drunkards nor slanderers nor swindlers will inherit the kingdom of God. And that is what some of you were. But you were washed, you were sanctified, you were justified in the name of the Lord Jesus Christ and by the Spirit of our God' (1 Corinthians 6:9-11).

Every Christian knows the truth of this. We know the blackness and depravity of our hearts, but now we are children of God, and it is all due to free grace. God is a God of grace. The gospel is a gospel of grace. The teachings of Scripture are doctrines of grace. And all this is embodied in the person of the Lord Jesus Christ. It is he who makes grace a reality to us. He brings grace, and his grace is proclaimed in the gospel.

The gospel will not pander to sinful man. It announces with uncompromising clarity that unless we are saved by grace, we cannot be saved at all. To say that we are saved by grace means, in the words of Dr Martyn Lloyd-Jones, 'Salvation is not in any sense God's response to anything in us. It is not something that we in any sense deserve or merit. The whole essence of the teaching at this point, and everywhere in all the New Testament, is that we have no sort or kind of right whatsoever to salvation, that the whole glory of salvation is, that though we deserved nothing but punishment and hell and banishment out of the sight of God to all eternity, yet God, of his own love and grace and wondrous mercy, has granted us this salvation. Now that is the entire meaning of this term grace.'[3] This means that salvation is a gift. It has to be because we cannot earn or purchase it. If God in grace did not give us salvation no one could be saved. That is how important grace is and that is why it is so precious.

Because we cannot be saved without grace it is imperative that grace be irresistible. This does not mean that God saves a man against his will; rather grace seeks to change the will, until the sinner wants salvation more than anything else. To quote

Dr Martyn Lloyd-Jones again, 'Not only is grace irresistible, it must be irresistible. For if grace were not irresistible no one would ever have been saved. That follows of necessity from the fact that we were dead spiritually and were at enmity to God, hating his truth. How can we be saved therefore? There is only one answer — the power of grace is irresistible.'[4]

Grace and law

John 1:17 tells us, 'The law was given through Moses; grace and truth came through Jesus Christ.' This does not mean that there was no grace in the Old Testament. 'Had the Old Testament times been times of stern, unbending law alone the whole complexion of the early world would have been vastly less cheerful than we find it to be in the ancient writings. There could have been no Abraham, friend of God; no David, man after God's own heart; no Samuel, no Isaiah, no Daniel. The eleventh chapter of Hebrews, that Westminster Abbey of the spiritually great of the Old Testament, would stand dark and tenantless. Grace made sainthood possible in Old Testament days just as it does today. No one was ever saved other than by grace, from Abel to the present moment.'[5] The paraphrase in the *Living Bible* of John 1:17 is totally wrong and misleading: 'For Moses gave us only the law with its rigid demands and merciless justice.' If there was only merciless justice in the Old Testament then none of the Old Testament people could have been saved. God was always a God of grace, and salvation was always by grace. It could be no other way. 'But grace and truth were fully revealed and perfectly exemplified when the Redeemer came to this earth, and died for his people upon the Cross. It is through Christ the Mediator alone that the grace of God flows to his elect.'[6]

The function of the law is not salvation. Its purpose is to show us our need of salvation. This it does by exposing sin.

Romans 5:20 says, 'The law was added so that the trespass might increase.' William Hendriksen comments that increase here means to magnify and thus expose. 'So the law acts as a magnifying glass. Such an instrument does not actually increase the number of dirty spots on a garment. It makes them stand out more clearly and reveals many more of them than one can see with the naked eye. Similarly the law causes sin to stand out in all its heinousness and ramifications.'[7] No one could be saved without this exposing and convicting work of the law, but once we are saved what part does the law play in our Christian living?

This was a problem that plagued the church in the New Testament era. There were two extreme reactions, legalism and antinomianism, and both were wrong. The legalist believed that grace was not enough and wanted to add his own works and efforts to it in order to earn salvation. This is the problem that Paul faced in his letter to the Galatians. The antinomian argued that because we are saved by grace it does not matter what sort of lives we live. These are the 'faith without works' people that the epistle of James opposes. They were changing 'the grace of our God into a licence for immorality' (Jude 4). 'Whereas the legalist so magnifies the law as to crowd out grace, the antinomian is so mesmerized by grace as to lose sight of the law as a rule of life.'[8]

The Christian saved by grace is to 'live a life of love, just as Christ loved us and gave himself up for us as a fragrant offering and sacrifice to God. But among you there must not be even a hint of sexual immorality, or any kind of impurity, or of greed, because these are improper for God's holy people' (Ephesians 5:2-3). Paul goes on in the same chapter to say we are to live as children of light (v.8), and we are to accomplish this by finding out what pleases the Lord (v.10) and doing it. Grace does not excuse us from keeping the moral law of God. Some Christians teach that grace has set us free from keeping the Ten Commandments. If you ask these Christians does that mean it is legitimate for the Christian to steal or kill or commit adultery, they will say no. In fact they will have to confess that we must keep all the commandments except one. The exception is the fourth, to keep the Sabbath day holy. This is very interesting thinking. Has grace really set us free from calling the Sabbath a delight and the Lord's holy day honourable? (Isaiah 58:13).

The life of grace is a life of freedom, but it is not a freedom to please ourselves and disobey God. Dr Packer lists three basic ways of being free under grace:[9]

1. Freedom from the hopeless necessity of trying to commend ourselves to God by perfect law-keeping.

2. Freedom from sin's dominion.

3. Freedom from bondage to fear.

14.
The patience of God

God's patience is the control he exercises over himself when his holiness and justice could be bringing judgement upon sinners. It is the patience of God that enables him to sustain great insults from men without immediately smiting them. Hence the biblical word used to describe this attribute is long-suffering. This is a very descriptive word; for a long time God suffers, or endures, or puts up with, the sin and rebellion of man.

God is not long-suffering because he has no choice and can do nothing about our sin. Often we are forced to be patient because circumstances are such that they are beyond our control. We have to grin and bear it. It is not so with God. There is no possible circumstance where he is not in control. God is omnipotent and it is interesting that often the Bible couples God's long-suffering with his power. 'What if God, choosing to show his wrath and make his power known, bore with great patience the objects of his wrath?' (Romans 9:22). 'The Lord is slow to anger and great in power' (Nahum 1:3).

Patience is not tolerance

Peter tells us that God's patience with sinners flows from his mercy. 'He is patient with you, not wanting anyone to perish, but everyone to come to repentance' (2 Peter 3:9). God takes

no delight in judgement, so in his grace and mercy he gives
sinners opportunity after opportunity to repent and seek
forgiveness. Scripture abounds with examples of this and
perhaps the most striking is the one to which Peter refers in the
third chapter of his second letter, the case of Noah and the
flood. From the time God announced his intention to flood the
world to the time it actually happened was a period of 120 years
(Genesis 6:3). Peter says that during this period Noah was a
preacher of righteousness (2 Peter 2:5). But the people would
not listen. God was long-suffering in spite of the strength of his
feelings. 'The Lord was grieved that he had made man on the
earth, and his heart was filled with pain.' For 120 years he was
patient but the people mistook patience for indifference. This
is a foolish attitude in man, and Ecclesiastes 8:11 warns us,
'When the sentence for a crime is not quickly carried out, the
hearts of the people are filled with schemes to do wrong.' There
is no excuse for this because God had warned very clearly in
Genesis 6 that his Spirit would not contend with man for ever.
Long-suffering is not endless. Patience will always eventually
give way to justice, and the flood finally came. The door of the
ark was shut and it was too late for repentance. God does not
want man to perish, but man is responsible for his sin, and if he
will not repent then he brings God's judgement upon himself.

The patience of God is a result of his love and mercy but the
holiness of God makes it inevitable that the patience will not
go on for ever. He holds back judgement for a while; that is the
pattern we see in Scripture. But patience is not tolerance. Even
in his patience God is long-suffering. Sin grieves him; he
suffers it, but never condones it.

At this point we need to look again at 2 Peter 3:9. Some use
this verse as an argument against divine judgement. The AV
translates it that God is 'not *willing* that any should perish'.
They argue, God's will is sovereign and must be done; therefore
none will perish, so all must go to heaven. The NIV translates
'will' as 'want' and the NASB as 'wish'. The comments of Dr

Lloyd-Jones on this one word are interesting: 'It seems to me that Peter's point is this, that a part of the explanation of what seems to us to be a delay is God's long-suffering. This we can be certain of, that God does not wish that any should perish (I did not say 'will', I said 'wish', for the word translated 'will' should really be translated 'wish'). Whatever God wills inevitably comes to pass — there is a difference between God willing and God wishing a thing, and what Peter says is that God does not wish that any should perish but that all should come to repentance. God takes no delight in the death of the ungodly; that is why, Peter says, he delays his action.'[1]

Delay and judgement

Though God delays his judgement because of his patience, that judgement will come. The fact that God is patient reminds us that divine judgement is not vindictive. God is slow to anger but he is angry with sin. The eventual judgement of sin is fully justified and God's patience makes man's guilt even worse. It removes any excuse. An example of this is God's dealings with Israel from the Passover onwards. Time after time he demonstrated his love for them, but it was not long before they were worshipping the golden calf. That was not a one-off episode because they continually turned to idols. God sent prophets to warn them but these were spurned. God remained patient but at times his judgement fell. The Babylonian exile was one of these times, but even then there was an element of patience as God sent prophets to the people to minister to them in Babylon.

All this served to show the hopelessness of man in sin. Man is always confident that he can cope and sort out the mess he has got into. God gave him century after century to show that he could not. But man is no wiser today. All the patience of God has revealed more guilt and heaped up more condemnation.

For 2,000 years the gospel of the Lord Jesus Christ has been offered to sinners. Man has no excuse.

Patience and the Christian

As Christians we thank God for his patience with us. How many times did we hear the gospel before we were saved? How many times did we reject the Lord Jesus? Peter says that we are to 'bear in mind that our Lord's patience means salvation' (2 Peter 3:15). And how many times since we were saved has God had to be patient with us? We need to thank God for his patience but we must not take it for granted.

In Isaiah 64 the prophet is praying for the Lord to return to his people. Why does he need to return? Because the sin of the redeemed grieved God and he was angry with them (v. 5), and he hid his face from them (v. 7). Verse 6 says, 'All of us have become like one who is unclean, and all our righteous acts are like filthy rags.' This is a verse we nearly always apply to unbelievers, but the context makes it clear that it is referring to God's people. The result of this sin was judgement (see vv. 9-11). Judgement, in the case of the redeemed, is not condemnation, because there is no condemnation for those in Christ, but none the less the anger of God on our sin can have very real present consequences. Sin needs to be repented of by the Christian continually. The patience of God should encourage repentance in us.

'May our meditation upon this divine exellency soften our hearts, make our consciences tender, and may we learn in the school of holy experience the patience of saints, namely, submission to the divine will and continuance in well doing.'[2]

15.
The glory of God

The phrase 'the glory of God', or 'the glory of the Lord', occurs in Scripture on many occasions but its exact meaning varies. For instance, when David in Psalm 19:1 says that 'The heavens declare the glory of God,' he obviously does not mean the same thing as Moses in Exodus 33:18 when he pleads with God, 'Show me your glory.' Psalm 19 teaches that the glory of God is obvious to all who have eyes to see, whereas in Exodus 33 a godly man like Moses has to plead to be allowed to see it.

We have seen that an attribute of God is whatever God has revealed as being true of himself. Hence we have studied his sovereignty, providence, holiness, and so on. To experience any of these attributes is a great blessing for any Christian, but I would suggest that the glory of the Lord is a revelation of all the divine attributes at once. The glory of the Lord is all that God is. It is his holiness, goodness, wisdom, and everything else. To see the glory of God is to see as much as it is possible for a human being to see of how utterly godlike and divine our God is. It is to realize as never before who God is. It is to see God in all his fulness and beauty.

A new start

The birth of the Lord Jesus Christ was heralded by the glory of the Lord shining upon a group of poor, ignorant, nameless shepherds on the hillside outside Bethlehem. These men were going about their normal business when suddenly they were confronted with the glory of the Lord (Luke 2:9). Their reaction was one of terror. Why? For the same reason that Solomon and his priests were immobilized when the glory of the Lord filled the temple in 2 Chronicles 5:14. All men, shepherds or kings, fear before such a revelation of divine glory. No one jumps up and down and shouts in the presence of the glory of the Lord.

That is a very sober lesson. Today there is a sad tendency for Christians to be too sure of themselves and to talk too glibly about God. This is because we are ignorant of the true nature of God. If we could but catch a real glimpse of his true glory how different we should be! Moses, in the cleft of the rock, covered by the hand of God while the Lord in all his glory passed by, saw only the back of God. But what a difference it made to him! His face was radiant and had to be covered with a veil (Exodus 34:29). He had seen the glory of God, and men knew it. The mark was upon him, and it was not a mark of arrogance or flippancy, but of godliness and authority.

The glory of the Lord is an awesome thing. No wonder the shepherds were afraid, but God does not reveal his glory in order to terrify men. The angel told the shepherds not to be afraid because there was great news for them and all people.

The revelation of God's glory is rare in Scripture and usually precedes a great work that God is about to start. In Exodus 33 there was a new start with the giving of the Ten Commandments. In 2 Chronicles a new and magnificent temple was being opened. But these are not to be compared with what God was beginning at Bethlehem. Nothing but the glory of the Lord could have introduced the birth of Jesus. It was not merely that a great company of angels were there; the Lord was there in all his glory. The incarnation was taking place and God was about to do a marvellous thing. God becoming man is the most staggering of all biblical truths. As Charles Wesley put it,

> Our God contracted to a span
> Incomprehensibly made man.

In the face of Christ

Isaiah the prophet refers to the glory of God:

> 'A voice of one calling:
> "In the desert prepare
>   the way for the Lord;
> Make straight in the wilderness
>   a highway for our God...
> And the glory of the Lord will be revealed,
>   and all mankind together will see it'
>
> (Isaiah 40:3-5).

Luke 3:4-6 makes it clear that the glory of the Lord about which the prophet is speaking is Jesus. Paul says much the same thing: 'For God, who said, "Let light shine out of darkness," made his light shine in our hearts to give us the light of the knowledge of the glory of God in the face of Christ' (2 Corinthians 4:6).

It is in Jesus that we see the glory of the Lord, and if we cannot see it in him we shall never see it. Jesus reveals God to us. He does not just tell us about God; he is God. At Bethlehem God was doing a new and amazing thing, and he is still doing it. He comes to hearts dark in sin to bring his light, and the purpose of this is to reveal to us the light of the knowledge of the glory of God in the face of Christ. He points us to Jesus and says, 'There is your only Saviour because he is my glory.' He takes us, as he took the shepherds, from Bethlehem to Calvary: 'Today in the town of David a Saviour has been born to you; he is Christ the Lord.' At Calvary the promised salvation became a reality as God reconciled sinners to himself.

We could not be Christians at all if we had not seen and believed this, but there is more of this glory in Jesus than the experience of salvation ever revealed to us. We need to acquaint ourselves more and more with the Lord Jesus Christ. Sin mars our vision, but the pure in heart will see God. If we want to see the glory of God, we need to order our lives so that we live for this glory. This means we need to fear God with a sense of awe and wonder, adore and worship him. Do you have a holy fear of offending God? Does your sin bother you because you know it grieves God?

We need to fill our lives with God: not merely with the things of God, but with God himself. We need to fill our homes with God. We need to fill our churches with God. That may sound strange, but it is not. How easy it is to come to church, sing the hymns, hear the sermon and have no real awareness of the presence of God! This is because we bring nothing with us. Do you take a sense of the presence of God to church with you? During the eighteenth-century revivals in Wales, crowds flocked to Llangeitho to hear Daniel Rowland preach. Many of them walked great distances for the privilege and they came with joy and anticipation. As they walked over the mountains they would be singing the praises of God. Daniel Rowland, hearing them approaching one day, said, 'Here they come, bringing the glory with them!'

Knowing God

Our greatest need today is to know God. Tozer quite rightly reminds us, 'The intellect can know God's attributes because these constitute that body of truth that can be known *about* God. The knowledge *of* God is for the spirit alone. Such knowledge comes not by intellect but by intuition. To know God in the scriptural meaning of the term is to enter into experience of him. It never means to know about.'[1]

Generally speaking, the evangelical Christian today has only a shallow experience of God. He is satisfied with religious candyfloss and chokes on doctrinal meat. He therefore has little knowledge about God, let alone an experimental knowledge of God. He needs to study the Word of God and to think. Tozer again reminds us, 'We cannot know God by thinking alone, but we can never know him very well without a lot of hard thinking.'[2]

The aim of this book is to get us thinking about God. But we must not stop there, but follow the advice of Spurgeon: 'Thank God for little grace, and ask him for great grace. He has given thee hope, ask for faith; and when he gives thee faith, ask for assurance; and when thou gettest assurance, ask for full assurance; and when thou hast obtained full assurance, ask for enjoyment; and when thou hast enjoyment, ask for glory itself; and he shall surely give it thee in his own appointed season.'

References

Chapter 1
1. A. W. Tozer, *The Knowledge of the Holy*, James Clarke, 1965, p.11.
2. A. W. Pink, *The Attributes of God*, Guardian Press, 1975 (taken from cover blurb).
3. C. H. Spurgeon, quoted by J. I. Packer, *Knowing God*, Hodder & Stoughton, 1975, pp.24-30.
4. Packer, *Knowing God*, pp.24-30.

Chapter 2
1. Pink, *Attributes of God*, p.32.
2. Packer, *Knowing God*, p.88.
3. J. M. Boice, *Foundations of the Christian Faith*, IVP, 1986, p.119.
4. C. H. Spurgeon, Sermon on Matthew 20:15, cited by Pink, *Attributes of God*, p. 32
5. Packer, *Knowing God*, p.92.

Chapter 3
1. C. H. Spurgeon, *The Early Years*, Banner of Truth, p.168.
2. W. Hendriksen, *Romans 9-16*, Banner of Truth, 1981, p.320.
3. J. I. Packer, Introductory Essay to *The Death of Death*, Banner of Truth, 1959, p.6.
4. Hendriksen, *Romans 9-16*, p. 320
5. S. Olyott, *The Gospel as it Really is*, Evangelical Press, 1987, p.87.

Chapter 4
1. Pink, *Attributes of God*, p.23.

2. D. M. Lloyd-Jones, *The Final Perseverance of the Saints,* Banner of Truth, 1975, p.237.
3. As above, p.236.
4. As above, p.239.
5. J. I. Packer, *God's Words,* IVP, 1981, p.187.

Chapter 5
1. Tozer, *Knowledge of the Holy,* p.112
2. A. W. Tozer, *Worship the Mission Jewel of the Evangelical Church,* Christian Publications Inc., pp.8-9.
3. Tozer, *Knowledge of the Holy,* p.114.
4. Pink, *Attributes of God,* p.44.
5. S. Charnock, *Discourses on the Existence and Attributes of God.*
6. Boice, *Foundations of the Christian Faith,* p.133.

Chapter 6
1. Boice, *Foundations of the Christian Faith,* pp.182-3.
2. Quoted in *A Golden Treasury,* Banner of Truth, 1977, p.230.

Chapter 7
1. Packer, *Knowing God,* p.82.
2. Pink, *Attributes of God,* p.37.
3. Packer, *Knowing God,* p.81.
4. As above, p.83.
5. Pink, *Attributes of God,* p.39.

Chapter 8
1. Tozer, *Knowledge of the Holy,* p.71.
2. Pink, *Attributes of God,* p.48.
3. Tozer, *Knowledge of the Holy,* p.73
4. Stephen Charnock, quoted by Pink, *Attributes of God,* p.46.
5. Tozer, *Paths to Power,* Oliphants, 1964, p.23.
6. C. H. Spurgeon, *The Attributes of God,* MacDonald, p.23.
7. Tozer, *Knowledge of the Holy,* p.73.

Chapter 9
1. Packer, *Knowing God,* p.96.
2. Tozer, *Knowledge of the Holy,* p. 68.
3. Packer, *Knowing God,* p.104.

Chapter 10
1. Manton, quoted by Pink, *Attributes of God*, p.57.
2. Tozer, *Knowledge of the Holy*, p.88.
3. Packer, *Knowing God*, pp. 179-80.
4. As above, p.182.
5. C. H. Spurgeon, quoted by Pink, *Attributes of God*, p.60.

Chapter 11
1. Pink, *Attributes of God*, p.83.
2. Packer, *Knowing God*, p.164.
3. J. Murray, *Redemption Accomplished and Applied*, Banner of Truth, 1961, p.117.
4. D. M. Lloyd-Jones, *The Gospel of God*, Banner of Truth, 1986, p.351.

Chapter 12
1. Tozer, *Knowledge of the Holy*, p.104.
2. Packer, *Knowing God*, p.135.
3. Pink, *Attributes of God*, p.78.
4. Tozer, *Knowledge of the Holy*, p.109.
5. Packer, *Knowing God*, pp.140-41.

Chapter 13
1. Packer, *Knowing God*, p.144.
2. Packer, *God's Words*, p.98.
3. D. M. Lloyd-Jones, *God's Way of Reconciliation*, EP, 1972, p.130.
4. D. M. Lloyd-Jones, *Assurance*, Banner of Truth, 1971, p.344.
5. Tozer, Knowledge of t*he Holy*, p.102.
6. Pink, *Attributes of God*, p.69.
7. Hendriksen, *Romans 1-8*, Banner of Truth, 1980, p.184.
8. Packer, *God's Words*, p.104.
9. As above, pp.106-7.

Chapter 14
1. D. M. Lloyd-Jones, *2 Peter*, Banner of Truth, 1983, p.181.
2. Pink, *Attributes of God*, p.64.

Chapter 15
1. Tozer, *Knowledge of the Holy*, p.46.
2. Tozer, *The Set of the Sail*, Kingsway, p.87.